C000157574

Author, Robin Welch, born in Bristol on election day July 5, 1945, has had an enthralling life full of personal, historical and professional experiences in many parts of the world. A grammar school boy, who experienced the sixties in the UK, played rugby in France, taught in Bristol and became an in-service inspector of schools in Botswana where he published the successful Macmillan Bolewsa Readers for the local primary schools.

His paternal grandfather, John Prichard, was a tailor in Gloucester, and is alleged to be the model for the Beatrix Potter classic, The Tailor of Gloucester. Unlike John Prichard, Robin did leave Gloucester and worked in education at various levels in Africa before entering the world of television and starting Africa's first pay TV channel in South Africa and later introducing sport as a valuable pay TV item.

Robin went on to work in Japan, Australia, the USA and Europe, advising on the establishment of pay TV channels, becoming a boxing promoter, a director of Leeds United, contracting many sports deals, and meeting many famous sports personalities. At the age of seventy-five, he is still involved in the TV sports business.

This book should intrigue all those post-war readers who thought of leaving, or did leave the UK in the 1970s for better opportunities throughout the globe.

BRISTOL (BRISTLE) BOY
&
THE TAILOR OF GLOUCESTER

Robin Welch

BRISTOL (BRISTLE) BOY
&
THE TAILOR OF GLOUCESTER

Vanguard Press

VANGUARD PAPERBACK

© Copyright 2023
Robin Welch

A CIP catalogue record for this title is
available from the British Library.

ISBN 978 1 80016 645 5

Vanguard Press is an imprint of
Pegasus Elliot Mackenzie Publishers Ltd.
www.pegasuspublishers.com

First Published in 2023

Vanguard Press
Sheraton House Castle Park
Cambridge England

Printed & Bound in Great Britain

To my wife, Maud, for her understanding of a writer's task. And the surviving Kingswood Grammar School boys: Jim, Steve, Pete and Rog. Thanks for the good times and camaraderie.

To my children, particularly Palesa for her typing skills and computer knowledge. Thanks to Tumelo for her memories of my father Adrian John Welch, born Prichard. To our other children Phetheho, Luzibo and Hazel — thanks for your patience.

The deputy headmistress of Kingswood Grammar School, Miss Morrison, spotted a young talent and nurtured it. Thanks Minnie!

Mark Williams in South Africa has provided much help with my television work and remained a true friend.

Mike Murphy, sadly deceased, provided amazing knowledge of sport and its celebrities.

Rodney Berman kept me sane during my TV boxing years.

Thanks to Professor Mughal who kept me alive in 2016.

To all my other colleagues in education and television, thanks for your help and usually good advice.

Lastly to the people of Botswana, thanks for four wonderful years that changed my life.

Johannesburg
15/02/2022

I came into the world on July 5, 1945: election day in UK, barely two months after VE day in May. I arrived in Bristol, eleven years after Grandpa Prichard, the Tailor of Gloucester, died in 1934. But more of him later.

I remember being frightened of the dark, dressed in my smock, and later sleeping in Granny's bed, seeing Germans in every shadow! Austerity Britain started in 1945 and lasted until 1954. I remember having to ration the small, rectangular orange juice bottle and other things I loved. Granny Summers, from Piddletrenthide in Dorset, lived in a council house just outside Bristol. She was born at the end of the Victorian reign.

Dad quit the fire brigade once the war was over and returned to teaching. Mother stayed at home looking after me. Bread and housing were scarce. Propitiously for me, London TV returned to twenty thousand pre-war viewers in 1946. I have no memory of the Great Freeze that tortured us all from January to March 1947. Hot summer: 1947. Power cuts. We stayed in a little suburban flat in Fishponds, Bristol, which still exists, over a doctor's surgery, until mid-1952. Was it the same doctor who told my mother not to let me eat bananas because they were rubbish? My birthdate marks my destiny and sure enough on July 5, 1948, the UK

National Health Service started. Doctors gave us medical checks at school, and dentists inflicted pain.

My local infant school in Fishponds was demolished in 1950. I remember sleeping afternoons, my blanket with its duck design and Jill, the first girl I fancied, sleeping next to me! The free milk they gave us tasted rotten when warm and was undrinkable in winter when frozen cream popped through the top.

Close by to the school was a tuck shop where a real monkey sat on top of a wall. I loved it and called it the Monkey House. I can also remember eating tinned snoek fish, a nutritious South African favourite. Apparently, Britain imported ten million tons. Little did I know how important South Africa would be later in my life.

Dad had purchased a war surplus army staff car (license KHY 192), which had seen service in the Western Sahara. Since it was painted in what seemed to be yellow camouflage paint, I called it the Flying Banana. It took us everywhere for many years, at a time when new cars were impossible to buy.

The Banana took us in early 1952 to a new rented flat in Downend, Bristol. A big place, in an old house, with trees and tree house, a garden, and Coop sports ground right in front. A kid's paradise. A new infant primary school for me in the Gloucestershire part of Bristol where I met up with other kids who were to become lifelong friends. I still visited Granny on

Sundays for roast beef and potatoes with beef cheaper than chicken at that time. The best taste ever.

Post-war Bristol was a grim place. You saw war damage and bomb sites until the early 1960s. I remember Broadmead replacing the old shopping centre, much against the wishes of local traders. There were new toy shops for me and the taste of Five Boys chocolate. My parents, I remember, smoked Woodbines, Craven A and Bristol cigarettes. I hated the smoky air. Made me cough and splutter all over the place.

Infant school passed by peacefully although Ms James and her great pair of knockers troubled me. The junior school in Downend was next to Dr W.G. Grace's cricket ground, and the church, and yes, his great grandchildren, Elizabeth and Joey went to school with me. Legend has it that W. G. Grace used to come to Downend in his glory days, put a sovereign on the wicket and say that anyone who could bowl and disturb the sovereign could have it!

Teachers told my mother — I was then eight — you will never do anything with that child! She was livid, and I determined to prove them wrong. I started reading avidly at about age nine. The library box used to arrive on a Friday, and I would gorge myself on Biggles, Jennings and Darbishire, Swallows and Amazons. Strangely, apart from P.E., I never did any team sports at the school. I dropped a kid who was bullying me on his head during PE. He never did that one again!

Granny Brain, one of my teachers, always smelt of stale perfume, cigarettes and peppermints. She tried to change me from left-handed to right-handed by beating me over the knuckles with a ruler. Luckily, she didn't succeed. As for the gypsy boy in my class, we called him Luke 'Stinky' Stevens. No politically correct sentiments or designations back then. Poor Luke kept disappearing with his endlessly wandering parents.

I arrived in fourth year juniors, not in the top class but being tutored for the deadly eleven plus. I remember saying tables over and over again, and enduring spelling tests. Handicraft on a Friday afternoon was always difficult for a left-handed person. I got whacked with a ruler by Mr McCulloch, and to this day I still can't cut straight, draw straight lines or use scissors. In fact, have to use scissors with my right hand. Apparently, Granny Brain's beatings worked only for scissors re-education.

When the headmaster got TB, we all thought we were dying. I spent a week in bed with high temperature. But I passed the eleven plus and got ready to go to Kingswood Grammar School, near Bristol. My delighted parents rewarded me with a new red Trent Tourist Raleigh bike. Twenty years later, I still had the thing. Outside school, I had become interested in everything: throwing mudballs through people's windows, putting fireworks in old ladies' dustbins, jumping out of windows and dropping earth on people's heads as they passed by our garden.

In those days, two old men played an interesting part in our lives. Mr Westley had a fantastic collection of old bikes, penny farthings and tricycles. We used to ride them after school, frightening local drivers to death. I found out later that the collection was sold for a fortune in the 1960s. Another old gent, Clarence Freeman, was a widower and Boer War veteran (1899–1902) who used to walk me and my best friend Jim Knight home from junior school. He would whistle and smoke at the same time! Mr Freeman gave Jim and me his Boer War rifle and bayonet. I wonder how we didn't get arrested as we played cowboys and Indians with real weapons. We also found, in his army webbing, a tin box stuffed with chocolate sent to the troops in 1900. This must have been about 1955, so the chocolate was then fifty years old. It still tasted good in the mouths of two ten-year-old boys. Sadly, whistling Clarrie passed away in the early 1960s. But not before he had told us more about the concentration camps in South Africa, the schools in the bush, the Indian Volunteer Bearers and the wonderful South African climate.

In the early fifties, my parents and I drove our old Austin Flying Banana to see our relatives: first Granny and Grandad on Mother's side. She was the one who made great Sunday roast and had a magical wartime bomb shelter in the garden. I would hide in it and throw apples at anybody approaching. The family loved listening out for radio messages from distant friends and relatives in Australia. Wilfred Pickles, Al Read and

Alma Cogan were all famous radio names of the times. As a family we were not cinema goers — although for some reason we did see the film 'Genevieve' in 1953. There was no television until 1953 when I sat in a neighbour's house, with my Coronation scrapbook from school and a beaker full of lemonade, watching the Queen get crowned in black and white. That was the last I saw of television until late 1959, when Dad bought a TV set and a white fridge. I had a lot of time for mischief and playing and reading. God knows where Mum stored the food before the fridge arrived.

There were no supermarkets in the 1950s. Groceries were delivered once a week by Mr Cadle in his small white van, meat by Mr Ford, and milk and bread daily by tradesmen. Close-by shops sold the rest, and the post office was handy for any letter or parcels. My best friend Jim lived near these shops, so it was always a good excuse to visit him when I was sent on errands. Life was so simple.

My godfather, Uncle Ted, actually one of Dad's cousins, ran a farm near Hartpury in Gloucester. In the early fifties, food was still in short supply, and it was always worth a visit for some meat and eggs and to hear him swearing about the church or his landlords or sometimes both in the same diatribe. Later on, at my confirmation, he assured me he was going to 'kick the fuckin' bishop' because the church was increasing his rent. Eventually he bought the farm and made a fortune. Old Ted was related to other cousins in Wales, and we got to know my cousin Richard and his parents who farmed near Whitland in Carmarthenshire. During one visit in autumn 1953, we found out that Cousin Richard, Dad's sister Phoebe, and her husband John Harries had disappeared from their farm near Pendine, South Wales. Eventually Superintendent Capstick of Scotland Yard found their bodies. A nephew, Ronald Harries, was found guilty of the killings and executed in Swansea on April 28, 1954. A good start to meeting long lost cousins. Dad always thought we were related to Dylan Thomas, which maybe explained our creative madness, but no proof ever emerged.

Cousin Richard's farm in 1953 had no electricity. Water ran through lead pipes, and the only toilet was in the garden. Or as my uncle said, you have to shit in the garden. But by golly, he produced the biggest vegetables I had ever seen. Magical days unfolded in the fields, chasing the cows, pulling calves from their mother's wombs, falling off horses, catching rabbits with a pet greyhound, Fly-catching trout in the streams, putting the milk churns in the cooling tank, making toast and eggs on the ever-burning Aga stove, auntie's scones and Welsh cakes, playing darts and the occasional visit to the Pembrokeshire coast for ice cream and a walk on the sands. Too cold to swim.

We had many distant relatives in west Wales, including Mad Mattie, who lived in an isolated farmhouse and decorated her walls with newspaper and went to the toilet in the garden, clutching a spade. All of them could cook sponges and Welsh cakes and so after afternoon visits, I was full to bursting with tea and Welsh patisserie.

Cousin Richard's father, Lawrence, was a pragmatic man who thought nothing of pushing the river bailiff into the river if he caught us fishing illegally for trout. Mysteriously, cars burnt out in the fields as their owners, including policemen, put in claims for insurance before the fire brigade put the fires out. Uncle Lawrence suffered for years from a strange illness that confined him to bed for long periods. No one could diagnose his problem. Celtic roots meant a soothsayer from Swansea, actually a train driver, was summoned to the house to rid Lawrence of evil spirits. A fire blazed in the parlour, and the devil was sent up the chimney in a cloud of black smoke. My ten-year-old brain could not comprehend this strange behaviour. Sadly, Uncle Lawrence passed away from the mysterious sickness, which turned out to be lead poisoning caused by the water pipes rather than Satan's work. My cousin and his mother, Doreen, who existed on tea and lemonade, seemed to be lead free.

Before he died, Uncle Lawrence spent much of his time ferrying his band of unmarried sisters-in-law and his mother-in-law around west Wales. His mother-in-law, or Mam, was a redoubtable Welsh matriarch who ruled her daughters with an iron rod from her high chair in the family home near Pendine. When she died, it emerged she had been going to two churches, Welsh

Methodist and Baptist. That's why she had two funerals and two wakes. Everybody was drunk for a week after her send-offs. A never to be forgotten event. Much of the catering was done by Cousin Willie, known as Willie the Fisher from the pub he ran in Whitland and from his other activity, poaching salmon. Until I went to Iceland later in life, Willie's fish was the best I had ever tasted.

Dad's mother, from west Wales, was to be the Tailor of Gloucester's first wife. Martha Ellen had four children with John Prichard: Adrian, my father, Leslie, Cristobel, (Chrissie for short), and Enid. Martha Ellen moved from Wales to Gloucester when she met and married John, who was to become famous as the Tailor of Gloucester in Beatrix Potter's book. In 1924, Granny Prichard left John, accusing him of cruelty, and moved to Horwich near Bolton in Lancashire, taking the two youngest children, Adrian and Enid, with her. There, Granny eventually married Joseph Welch. Our little old Austin army surplus car would transport us to Lancashire to see the other side of the family, now called Welch.

Bolton, in the early fifties, was a bustling, friendly but grimy place, still recovering from the war and trying to boost its heavy engineering, coal mining and textiles industries. People seemed so much more friendly than in Bristol. Always in each other's houses, helping, gossiping, drinking tea. I can remember hearing the clump of clogs in the street as miners and factory workers passed by the house early in the morning; the whistle of steam trains at the Railway Works; people smoking and coughing in the street; and the clop, clop of the horse and cart delivering the milk. Also going on fishing expeditions to local streams to catch sticklebacks, the smell of fish and chips in many streets, Greenhalgh's meat and potato pies and for the first time drinking Vimto, Sarsaparilla and Burdock Nectar from the north, not available in the south. I think I had my first Coca Cola as well during one of these trips from Bristol to the north. No motorways then. The journey took at least six hours.

Granny Welch had survived the late twenties, thirties, forties and early fifties doing a variety of jobs and becoming a councillor, mayor and prospective Labour MP. Tragically, she was to die of a botched operation in 1958. She once took me to meet her friend, Leslie Lever, later a socialist minister, at Ringway Airport, Manchester. He owned his own aeroplane and took me on my enthralling first flight. But I had one problem. Granny by then was so very corpulent, I asked her if the plane could take us all into the air. Everybody laughed, but I was very serious.

Joseph Welch, whom I thought was my grandfather (the Prichard link was still a family secret), had survived World War I and worked at De Havilland Aircraft as a clerk. He always wore a trilby hat and spent his after-hours at the pub. At night I could hear him peeing in the chamber pot under the bed to avoid trekking to the downstairs toilet. He loved tippling pints and whisky chasers and going on holiday to the Isle of Man, where the pubs were open all day! The other children of the Tailor of Gloucester were Leslie, Cristobel and Enid who lived with her mother and family in Lancashire. Dad's brother, Uncle Leslie, visited us from time to time when I was a child and always seemed strange. Only later did I discover he had been prone to nervous breakdowns throughout his life. As his daughter said to me, he was crackers till the end! Dad's other sister, Cristobel, eventually lived near Stroud in Gloucestershire, and had similar mental demons. She stayed with us for a while, and I remember coming home from school to find a terrible smell of gas in the house. She had tried to kill herself, but luckily failed. Hard to understand for a six-year-old for whom death meant nothing.

Cousin Gwenda, from Lancashire, who was studying at Bristol University, came to stay at our house in early 1950. So did a French girl called Christine, later to marry my Uncle Leo, my mother's brother. Apparently, I ruined their courting by following them and appearing in unexpected places at tricky moments. I suppose I was picking up tips for later life.

Back in Bristol, Dad was bringing up Joey the pig, as back in 1952. Britain was short of food. Unfortunately, when Joe reached the correct weight for slaughter, he became ill. Dad came rushing home from school to make sure Joey didn't die before arriving at the abattoir. It looks like he made it, although I was never happy with bacon after that. My Welsh corgi pup, Rusty, arrived from my cousin's farm and bit my dad every time he tried to give me a hiding. He was a well-trained little dog who watched me play with my Hornby clockwork train set. My friend Jim inherited an electric train set from his brother, and I was very envious.

During my later junior school days, there were holidays in caravans with grandparents, usually windy and wet, especially one week on Chesil Beach near Weymouth where I nearly drowned, and Dad had an attack of boils. Don't know if the two were related.

On another trip we went to the Isle of Man. My Uncle Mike, from my mother's side, got a telegram during our stay in a Douglas bed and breakfast, calling him up for service during the Suez Crisis of 1956. He had to rush back and waste three months under canvas in Malta. The rest of us took a boat trip to Belfast, Northern Ireland. The roughest seas I had ever seen. Mountainous waves. Granny lost her false teeth overboard, and I was sick as a dog. Can't remember much of Belfast but it seemed very poor. Lots of horses pulling carriages. Never been back since.

My mother's mother, Granny Summers, came from Dorset. One fine summer Saturday, we joined a group of Bristolians in a charabanc going to a summer fete near Piddletrenthide. On board, amateur singers, dancers and tap dancers, all from Bristol, lit up the event. Tea, lemonade, cakes, balloons, model aeroplanes. It was just like going back to a church fete of the twenties. Plenty of vicars and widows. It seemed to me to be like a trip to an unknown rural England of the past.

As I started to read well towards the end of junior school, I took a look at Dad's daily newspaper, the News Chronicle. I remember the odd headline: the sinking of SS Andrea Doria in 1956, when sixteen hundred people were saved off the American coast. Don't forget — no TV in our house then, so newspapers were everything. Comics such as the Eagle, Topper, Beaver, Beano and Dandy fascinated and entertained me and my friends in between bouts of soccer in the local park. I joined Uncle Bob's club in the Bristol Evening Post and got a letter of congratulations on my birthday. Great news for a ten-year-old to receive a letter addressed to Master Robin Welch. I had a friend called John Bates. He must have hated it when he received his letter addressed to Master J. Bates!

In late 1955, instead of joining the scouts, I signed onto the Junior Training Corps (JTC) of the Church Lads Brigade in Downend. The scouts were founded in the UK by Baden Powell and by 1908 had a troop in South Africa. Powell defended Mafeking in 1899/90 and later on I was to live in modern day Mahikeng. The JTC gave me five wonderful years of marching, collecting insects and plants, games, model aeroplane making, church visits and boys' fun. We used to meet in our hut, go on parade, and then split into groups for

23

various activities. I remember playing cricket and making a spectacular drive, only to stand up covered in dog shit. Someone had forgotten to clean the cricket pitch.

Summertime also meant watching cricket at Downend Cricket Ground, the home of W.G. Grace and the Coop ground, near where I lived. I saw great Gloucestershire players of the era: David Allen, Arthur Milton, the last of the double internationals in cricket and soccer and John Mortimore.

Happy days came in the late fifties, when we finally got television. I returned home for a glass of lemonade and a piece of fruit cake and watched Billy Bunter on the small black and white screen. 'Bend over, you wretched boy!' was a catch phrase in the Billy Bunter show and certainly would not be allowed now. It was a rather apposite phrase for the time, when homosexuality was still well under the public consciousness and unknown to me. The JTC in my area was run by several fellows later accused of child molestation. Always wondered why my mother kept asking me if any strange men had touched me.

By the mid-1950s, even with its bomb sites, Bristol was looking better. Rationing finished in July 1954. Despite my doctor, I must have eaten plenty of bananas by then! Bristolians were considered slow by others because of their accent. Apparently, when the Great Western Railways opened their line to Bristol in 1841, Bristol time was considered ten minutes different from

London's. My friend Jim used to take me to the former French prison in Fishponds, which had become Manor Park mental hospital. We would watch cricket there and mingle with the so-called mad patients who were allowed out of their rooms. Both Methodism and Quakerism were strong in Bristol at this time. But this did not even slow down prodigious drinking, as new pubs opened in the suburbs and war-damaged pubs were reopened or replaced.

Soccer was big in Bristol, and I was a Bristol Rovers fan or Gashead. The nickname derived from the gasometers that surrounded the original ground at Eastville. Most of the old ground now houses IKEA.

Dad, by now a headmaster in Bristol, would take me to Rovers, along with friend Uncle Len Batten, who was a director of a timber firm in Bristol docks. I remember seeing Rovers vs. Preston on Jan 30, 1960, FA Cup fourth round tie with Tom Finney playing. What a treat! The ground had thirty-eight thousand, four hundred and seventy-two people! Rovers struggle to get eight thousand today. This part of my youth sparked my lifelong interest in soccer which certainly helped me with my eventual career in television.

Fry's chocolate, the Kleen-eze man, the Corona lemonade man, Harveys Bristol Cream, Cabot Tower, Bristol Aircraft Corporation (BAC), Bristol Pottery, Douglas Motorcycles, Wills Tobacco, Aust Ferry to Wales, Babycham and Britvic Orange, Smiths Crisps: these were all memorable iconic tags for me in the fifties and sixties. So many memories of visits, sights, sounds and tastes. Not forgetting Reg, the part-time hairdresser who gave me a crew cut for the first time. His wife had a beard, strange for a hairdresser's wife, and Reg was always offering his gentlemen clients something for the weekend. Only later did I understand he was talking about condoms!

As I turned eleven, I became interested in collecting cigarette packets and trainspotting. I can remember following one gentleman down the road, hoping he would drop his Passing Cloud cigarette packet as that was a rare item then. Another person smoked Balkan Sobranie which had a pungent sweet smell so good that it was worthwhile walking behind him to get a whiff of the perfumes. My parents smoked horrible Woodbines, Players and Craven A. Aunty Enid in Lancashire smoked full strength Capstans and if she hadn't stopped, I'm sure she would've coughed herself to death. Made my breakfast, bacon and eggs, taste terrible.

As I went to grammar school, I gained a degree of independence as I had to ride the bus to school and from now on was able to visit various local train stations to cop or write down the names and numbers of trains all over the country. Exciting stuff, spotting Castles, Kings, Britannias, Granges, Manors and Jubilees, all tabulated in books by a publisher called Ian Allen. I soon visited locomotive sheds in Bath, Gloucester and Swindon with friends from school. Equipped with books, pens, raincoats, sandwiches and fruit, we were a happy band, even riding on local trains in the Bristol area and keeping an eye out for the station master. Sometimes we forgot to buy our platform tickets. Trainspotting kept me going till about 1960, when rugby and girls started to take up too much time. I still have my trainspotting books in the attic till this day.

Occasionally I would ride with Dad in his Ford Popular (the Austin Flying banana had now retired) to visit a sprightly old lady born in the 1880s in Kingswood, Bristol. Liza, or Mrs Webbley, as she was respectfully known, had been Dad's landlady in the 1930s when he had first come to teach in Bristol. She was a delightful, half blind old woman who left me her Victoria scrapbook and a gold coin. Her house was full of antique furniture and vases, and in the back garden a fine array of old chimney pots. These were filled with soot from her chimney and in them she produced fantastic rhubarb. Sometimes she gave me a rhubarb pie to take home. She lived until she was ninety, and like my grandmother was a great link to the Victorian period. I used to pull legs by saying that I had just heard that Mahikeng in South Africa was relieved during the Boer War. Years later in Mahikeng itself, I was to meet a lady who had sat on Baden-Powell's knee!

At the end of August 1956, I walked from our flat to the bus stop, showed the conductor my new pass, and boarded the 97 for Kingswood Grammar School, near Warmley, Bristol. Just eleven years of age I was probably bright but immature and found it hard to settle for the first six months. As I was later to discover from Hoggart's 'Uses of Literacy', I was the 'working-class child emotionally uprooted from their class, often under the stimulus of a stronger critical intelligence or imagination. And who can never escape from an underlying sense of some unease'.

This lack of confidence dogged me for many years. It probably affected my father as well. He came from the depression and wanted nothing more than a steady job, and a pension. Looking back, grammar school pupils often had the knowledge but not the social skills and business acumen of their private or public-school peers. How could we, when dinnertime table talk consisted of school timetables, lathes, woodworking, building, nursing and social care? No business or law conversations, which were difficult to pick up later as I found out during my career. At least there were girls in mixed grammar schools. My experiences stood me in good stead later at college when a public schoolboy type asked me how to get off with girls. Clearly, he had never got close to a female! I told him you had to get close to them and hold their breasts! He did! So, William, how did you get on? She slapped my face and kicked me in the balls, he said. Maybe one point scored for the grammar school boys.

It was about this time that I was becoming aware of pop music, especially Radio Luxembourg, and listened at night to the whooshing reception from far away. Later of course, with the arrival of transistor radios, I listened to it late into the night under the bed clothes. Radio Luxembourg transmitted music programmes with advertising and circumvented the then BBC policy of no broadcast commercial sponsors. One of the advertisers was Horace Batchelor who promoted his famous betting Infra Draw Method. Horace was based in a small town just outside Bristol. Every night he annoyed the local Bristolian listeners, with his pedantic spelling out of K-E-Y-N-S-H-A-M. Later on, the Bonzo Dog Doo-Dah Band even called an album Keynsham.

The BBC finally realised that pop music was here to stay, and during mid-1957 introduced the Saturday Club on the Light Programme — compulsive listening on my parents' big Bush radio in the flat. At the same time, 'Rock around the Clock' by Bill Haley and the Comets got us all rocking and rolling. I and my friend Jim spun platters on the record player that belonged to his brother Peter, who was ten years older than us. Pete introduced us to jazz and Jelly Roll Morton. We had some great times listening to records in Jim's back room and trying to do our early homework at the same time. Peter Knight also had an air rifle, and we soon found out how to use it, from shooting birds to taking pot-shots at the nurses in the hospital next door, inducing them to drop their trays. Don't know how we got away with it! We were also good at blasting holes in the neighbours' sheets hanging on the clotheslines. Naughty buggers!

My new school, Kingswood Grammar was locally known as the Cowsheds. New pupils were herded into the hall and divided into classes with a class teacher. My class was called 1WY, after Miss Wycherley, a handsome, enormously bosomed lady in her late fifties, who taught English. One or two familiar faces from junior school were in my group, but the rest of my friends were spread around the other first year classes. This school would be my home for the next eight years and would take me from childhood to manhood. I was an immature eleven-year-old and at the beginning found it hard to settle.

I was in love with Gill, who lived near my home and rode down to see her on my new bike every evening.

My early efforts at homework were very poor. Luckily for me, Miss Morrison, a white-haired rotund little lady in her fifties, the deputy headmistress, nicknamed Minnie by the pupils, took me in hand. She must have realised there was some ability and goodness in me and gave me a good talking-to. From then on, I slowly settled down and enjoyed my studies and seemed to be equally good at arts and sciences.

The school was run-on public-school lines by headmaster Mr C.N. Ridley, an Oxbridge graduate and former housemaster from Harrow. The school opened in the 1920s and Mr Ridley was only its second headmaster. A strongly disciplined house system was in force. Girls played hockey in the winter and tennis and athletics in the summer whilst the boys played rugby and cricket and athletics. Soccer was a ruffian's game and until just before the end of my sixth form days, was taboo. The system introduced me to rugby. It was my first team game as there was none at my junior school. Rugby came to play a very important part in my life from that moment on.

School assemblies were compulsory most days, and every term finished with the jingoistic song, 'Jerusalem' by William Blake. 'And did those feet in ancient time, Walk upon England's mountain green?' And so it went on with: 'countenance divine', 'Satanic mills', 'chariot of fire'! Don't think any of us understood these words and were more interested in getting out of the assembly hall.

C.N. Ridley was regarded as snooty and aloof, but he ran the school at a high academic level and dragged us ordinary kids along. Many pupils disliked him, but as I got older and became a prefect, I realised what a dedicated educationist and wise person he was. Only after he had retired did we discover he had been a working-class Sheffield boy who earned a scholarship to university, married a rich lady and along with his own children, brought up a student at the school who had lost his parents. They probably don't make them like him any more.

Slowly, as summers came and went, I got to know teachers from the various disciplines. They all had nicknames. Bunny Austin, infamous for his rabbit punch to the neck, was our physics teacher. Jimmy Wilde, the PE and games teacher, had a mean tennis shoe, or dap that left an imprint on your bottom if he caught you misbehaving. Fishy Salmon, the chemistry teacher, had been a pupil at the school when it opened in the 1920s and had come back to teach after graduation. Don't think he knew any other life. The irascible Eric Hilton: music teacher extraordinaire for some, but I transferred to geography in year three, as I was a hopeless case. Mr Wintour, Frosty Wintour to us, was the head of French. The adorable Miss Richards, Latin mistress: had a real crush on her. And Bony Britton, an English teacher who could no longer control us. One day we made a chair of very light balsa wood and put it at the front of the class. Bony would normally storm into the room and in an effort to dampen the mayhem in front of him would pick up the nearest chair and throw it to the ground. Of course, this time the chair shattered into hundreds of pieces and thirty-odd kids collapsed with howls of laughter.

Back at home, we were still in the flat overlooking the Coop Cricket Ground in Downend. Dad had become headmaster of another school in Bristol and in 1960, Mum would launch herself as a Tupperware representative. But before that event, Dad made the momentous decision to buy a fridge, or Frigidaire, and a TV set, black and white of course! The cinemas were doing well in the late fifties, showing movies such as 'The Red Balloon', 'The Inn of the Sixth Happiness' and 'The Hound of the Baskervilles'. At our local cinema, the Vandyke, there was even a children's movie club on Saturday mornings, but I did not go to that. Dad made his move because of the advent of commercial television in the west of England. The BBC had been transmitting in our region since the early fifties, but the arrival of Television Wales and the West in January 1958 finally pushed Dad over the edge, despite Lord Reith of the BBC claiming that the introduction of commercial television would be a national disaster comparable to dog racing, smallpox and bubonic plague! It certainly wasn't a national disaster. Local news was good; Sunday Night at the London Palladium was a treat. The Army Game, and later Bootsie and Snudge, were fun and different from the BBC shows. And of course, we soon got the American shows like Wagon Train. A new world of sights and sounds had been opened.

As I approached my early teens, homework started to get heavy, and TV viewing was competition for that damned homework book my parents had to sign every night. My friend Jim had inherited an electric train from his brother, so my clockwork Hornby got put outside, and Jim's train took some of my time. Jim and I also went to play in a nearby park and one day an accident happened. We were crawling along the edge of a crumbling cliff above the river, pretending to be Indians on patrol, when Jim suddenly disappeared in front of me. The edge of the cliff had collapsed, and Jim fell about twenty feet. I climbed down to him, and luckily, he was not unconscious. As he groaned about pains in his left arm and back, I managed to lift him up, got him on my back and walked about half a mile to get help. He had broken his arm and damaged vertebrae in his back. His dad blamed me for the accident. I thought this was not fair, as I had just saved him. Jim spent time in hospital and then on a wooden mattress at home. His parents were nurses and luckily, he recovered. We are still friends.

By my fourth year at grammar school, I was doing well academically and was fast-tracked to do some 'O' levels in June 1960, when I was still only fourteen years old. I managed to pass some subjects but decided to do the remaining ones in June 1961. By then I was nearly fifteen, the hormones were bouncing, and I was mad for rugby and playing the occasional game for the school's second team. Mum now had her fridge and foods such as fish fingers and frozen peas now appeared in time for our evening meal. I still like them both!

Until 1960 at least, Kingswood Grammar School was all white, except for one Mike Robinson, who was a friend. In these often-racist times, it was hard to believe no one ever mentioned Mike's colour. Only many years later did one of my friends remind me of Mike and say, you must remember him, the black guy! My parents were very tolerant of people of different races and religions, and thank goodness I inherited their openness from them. My father's only prejudice was against the Japanese, who had cruelly tortured some of his friends during the war. Until near the end of his life, he refused to buy anything Japanese and only bought a

Nissan car when he found it was made in Sunderland, UK!

School and home life continued to be a pleasure well into late 1959 and early 1960. Rabbits bred in my garden, we shot catapults in the air, and I found my pet tortoise to put it into a box for winter hibernation. School doctors, who were still around, vaccinated us against polio and held us down as they gave us anti-tuberculosis shots (a disease still widespread in Britain). Vaccination involved one hell of a bubble on the skin that festered for months. Many friends came back in tears, but at least we had the certificate to prove the pain. Sex education was in its infancy, and Mr Williams' biology classes gave us some talks while showing us the results of illicit sex if we ventured down the slippery slope, as he called it. Nothing about condoms, the only device available, well before the pill. Strangely, in my teenage years I can only remember one girl at school getting pregnant and one other girl, a vicar's daughter and friend, having a child. Either we were not doing it through fear or were just lucky.

Another teacher, Mr Williams Woodwork, liked hitting us on the back of the head. At the age of thirteen or fourteen, I was developing a keen sense of justice and decided to pay him back. By the way, woodwork and metalwork were supposed to be a treat for the academically able. However, for most of us, it was more like a nightmare! One autumn day Williams Woodwork fired up the electric forge so we could make a soup ladle and handle. The forge had a handle to increase the air supply and make the coals hotter. As Mr Williams walked by, a vengeful Welch pushed the air handle to maximum and covered Mr Williams with red hot sparks. The class collapsed with laughter, and Williams ran away swearing and patting his coat to extinguish the smouldering sleeves and lapels. Once his charred jacket stopped burning, he chased me around the room, gave me a good leathering and put me on detention for weeks. Ah, but revenge was sweet against the nicotine-stained-fingered Welshman who later wrongly accused me of jumping out of a school window.

I must have been going through a naughty anti-social period in 1959/1960. One summer afternoon, my friends Steve and Jim and I stripped naked our other friend Andrew and threw him out onto the garden of Steve's house, which was right next to a bus stop. Steve had a phone in his house then, as did I, and subscriber trunk dialling had come to Bristol in 1958. So, we used this modern device to phone the telephone box next to the bus stop and ask any ladies waiting for the bus if they could see a naked man. You can imagine their comments when they answered the phone. Andrew, of course, was still trying to get back into the house! That same Steve, a trumpet player, later did vacation work for a lawnmower company at the annual Bristol Flower Show on the Downs. He plugged a cork into the exhaust pipe of one of the petrol lawnmowers, kick started it and the resulting explosion, as the cork shot out of the exhaust pipe, brought the show to a halt. For twenty minutes or so it seemed like a terrorist attack.

As a family, we continued our trips to Wales and Lancashire. One day, Cousin Richard in Wales was found drunk in the fields after imbibing all the beer intended for the workers during harvest time. His mother was furious, but we helped put it right by helping Uncle Lawrence, Richard's dad, to deliver a calf stuck in its mother's vagina. It was a messy business, plenty of blood and shit. A rope was attached to the calf's back legs, and three of us pulled the poor beast from its mother's birthing canal. The effort was worth it. Uncle Lawrence rewarded us with excellent Welsh farm food, including vegetables fertilised by human excrement from the family's prolific garden.

At that time, Dad was a part time trade union representative for the National Association of Schoolmasters (NAS) and a lifetime socialist like his mother and sister. On trips to Lancashire, we would often go into the Horwich Labour Club, me sitting in the corner with a Britvic Orange, and Dad and Grandad with a pint and whisky chaser. It was fascinating to hear the discussions of the working folk and their disdain for the Conservative Club just up the road. The Labour Club continued until the 1970s when it filed for bankruptcy! At the final committee meeting, apparently some wag said, if the club has gone bust, let's have a party to celebrate. Something wrong with the logic there.

My mother's elder brother Leo had met and married a French girl, of Polish extraction, in the very early 1950s. Paris, according to my uncle, was Pickwickian then and had still not recovered from the war. Leo and Christine began to live in England where he was a scientist with the Bristol Aircraft Corporation, and she was a teacher. Christine had a doctor in Paris, a Polish refugee who had a son, Patrice Fingerhut. He came to visit us in Bristol in 1959 and I stayed with them in the summer of 1960. So began a lifelong friendship.

France in 1960 was still struggling to recover from World War II which had only ended fifteen years before. Many of the towns and villages were still damaged, and there were no autoroutes or motorways. My friend's parents met me at Le Bourget Airport, no Charles de Gaulle then, and took me to their house in suburban Paris for the night. My first flight had been from Bristol to Paris in an old Dakota or DC3. It seemed to fly uphill, or at an angle it seemed to me, and that along with excitement had made me tired. Nevertheless, my hosts insisted we have a steak dinner in the legendary Coupole restaurant on Boulevard Montparnasse in Paris: full of well-dressed people, all smoking pungent Gitanes cigarettes. I tried to order a well-cooked steak in my best sixteen-year-old 'O' level French and I got five hundred grammes of pink beef. It went back five times to the kitchen, before accompanied by the chef, it came back in a condition I found edible. The chef asked my friends if this Englishman really liked having his steak cooked like an old boot! It took me many years before I could eat bloody steak in the French way.

Next day, we set off from Paris to drive to Royan on the French Atlantic coast. This was to be our first stop en route for Hossegor in the Landes region of the south west. My friend's father, Dr Fingerhut, was a Polish exile who had settled and married in France after the war. He was in touch with a network of French based Poles, one of whom was our host for that stopover in Royan. This gentleman owned a correspondence school based in Royan and had obviously prospered. The house, on the top of a cliff, was magnificent. I had my own bedroom and en suite bathroom. Unbelievable for a boy from a modest flat in Bristol. Passers-by tried to look into the house and see the paintings and furniture. I imagined myself to be on a movie set.

I walked down the steps to the beach in the early evening, sat down on a rock and started to cry. I hadn't realised I was homesick! After a couple of minutes, I pulled myself together and said to myself, you must never again be homesick. You are always fine wherever you are at that moment. This feeling has served me well wherever I have been in life, apart from jail in Angola! But that's another story.

Next day we drove on to our final destination, Villa Bazterzabal in Hossegor, south west France. My friends had a summer home and spent three months of school holidays in their villa amongst the pine trees, very close to the lagoon. What a place! Warm days and nights, the ocean, discovering French food, fishing, cycling, musical evenings in the open air, movies and live shows. During subsequent visits to Hossegor in 1963 and 1964, I saw the Harlem Globetrotters basketball team, Richard Bergmann, the world champion table tennis player and Cliff Richard in 'Summer Holiday'. Super memories. I even got used to eating yoghurt, then regarded as health freak food in Britain, if you could find it.

My friends, the Fingerhuts, often invited neighbours and friends for an aperitif. One afternoon I looked up and saw a beautiful sun-tanned girl gliding into the house. Sophie, the daughter of a shoe manufacturer, smiled at me. She was to be my Françoise Hardy, the iconic yé-yé pop singer every Englishman lusted after. I pursued her relentlessly on the beach, amongst the pine trees, on my aged bicycle during country rides, but it was not to be. There would be other French girls later in life.

Patrice and I slept in the garage which had been converted into a bedroom suitable for two male teenagers. During the warm summer nights, I would often wake up and hear a *cri cri* sound. Being a boy from Bristol, I had never heard this sound before, yet I was aware of the French Algerian war and thought I was hearing terrorists placing explosives in Hossegor. My hosts eventually explained to this bumpkin from Bristol that it was the sound of cicadas in the pine trees. Just as well I did not show Sophie how stupid I was!

A magical summer came to an end, and I returned to Bristol and Kingswood Grammar School, having just completed four 'O' levels, and settled down to do more subjects, and decide if I was an art or science man. Girls were becoming more interesting but mainly confined to a quick kiss on someone's settee or a hurried grope at a party. No alcohol yet, and certainly no drugs!

At this time, I befriended a fellow who had come to Bristol from the north of England. Raymond P. was partially disabled, had a great smile, a fine sense of humour and a huge interest in radio. He had his own illegal radio transmitter. Too young to get a licence, he chatted happily to people all over the world. Raymond P. and his school friend Russell T. taught themselves morse code so they could transmit in secret but also have conversations in class without the teacher, or their fellows, being able to eavesdrop. Russell became known as Tappy T. He and Raymond constantly went around making dit dit da sounds, to the annoyance of everybody else.

As Raymond's knowledge of radio and transmissions grew more extensive, and the power of his radio set increased, he embarked upon an ingenious plan. He targeted the BBC Light Programme, the BBC radio station broadcasting entertainment and music. Raymond contrived to block it out from the northern suburb of Bristol where he lived. After an avalanche of complaints from Light Programme-less listeners, Raymond was eventually tracked down by the General Post Office of the time and taken to the local police station for a severe reprimand and warning. What a gas! He achieved something even the Germans could not do.

By the end of June 1961, I had completed more 'O' levels and was set for the sixth form and 'A' levels from September. Eventually it was decided I would do history, geography and French and not science subjects. Can't really remember why! Before the sixth form and during the summer holidays, one more treat. A school visit to Austria in July 1961.

Thirty-nine boys and girls travelled by boat and train to Otz, in the Austrian Alps. We met American soldiers who could hardly speak English, jumped off freezing chair lifts, and stole all of the tickets from our teachers' mattresses, later to be returned after many threats. Peter W., one of my lifelong friends, fell in love, and I woke up on top of a young lady after drinking too much cherry brandy! Can't remember her name now.

Slowly the boyhood interests such as trainspotting, making Airfix model kits, jumping out of the high windows of our flat with a so-called safety rope, and bike riding, began to fade in favour of girls and rugby, although trainspotting, with its travel to dirty old stations and the magic of steam engines as they wheezed and clattered past continued to challenge our hormones. Oddly named stations such as Bath Green Park, Mangotsfield, Staple Hill, Temple Meads and Stroud occupied many Saturday afternoons as we tried to see or cop every steam train in our region. Never saw any girl trainspotting though! I love the story of the Great Western Railway or GWR, opening its line to Bristol in 1841, and regarding Bristol as ten minutes different in time from London! Maybe nothing has changed.

Studies for 'A' levels progressed well; still no drugs in school at that time. Eighteen was the legal age in a pub and no one really knew how to have sex with a girl. There was a lot of groping and kissing but no end result. Used condoms found in the park were regarded as party balloons. At sixteen, some friends had motorbikes, but I was left on a push bike as my mother threatened to kill herself if ever I drove one. I've never had one to this day and rarely have even sat on them.

Slowly the idea came to me, as I approached seventeen, that driving was not far away. No written tests or exams in those days, you just got in the car and tried to drive off. A frightening experience with manual transmission for me, the learner driver, and my father mentoring. Much swearing and near misses of trucks and buses, some of which must have been driven by Eddie J., a near neighbour, who upon reflection must have been afflicted by prostate problems: he was constantly rushing for his next pee!

Dad had a series of cars after the Flying Banana, and I learnt on his latest beauty, an Austin A35, which made a strange klonking noise as you went round a tight bend. The car frightened old ladies, mothers and babies, vicars, school crossing ladies and workmen on bikes. I terrorised these people as I learnt to drive. My mounting kerbs and backing into heaps of gravel also tested Dad's patience. Once, driving away from a heap of stones, the exhaust pipe blasted a vicious shower of pebbles into the car behind me, breaking its headlight. Angry confrontation ensued between my dad and the owner of the vehicle.

Of course, I was not the only one learning to drive, giving parents heart attacks. My friend Garth crashed through a hedge in a park. He was trapped in a vast circle of privet hedges that sprang up behind him. The only way to get out was to do the same thing in reverse! His mother was puce with anger.

Eventually, the day of the driving test arrived: December 1962. I was seventeen and a half years old. It snowed that day, and I expected the test to be postponed. But no, the tester was determined to go ahead. He asked me a few highway code questions and then made me drive along snowy, icy roads, suddenly asking me to do an emergency stop on a very slippery hill. I asked him if he was mad. Trying to obey him, I braked hard. The car skidded but I controlled it and brought it to a stop. That's enough, he said. Oh God, I failed, I thought. No, he said that was very good in difficult conditions; you've passed. Let's go back to the test centre.

So, freedom to drive a car at last. Little did I know that Dad had no intention of lending me the vehicle and kept refusing me until he was eighty and I was fifty!

Several of my lifelong friends, Brian and Phred, real name Peter, had part time jobs and managed to buy old Austin Sevens. These guys were technically minded and even at seventeen or eighteen could repair anything. We used to take trips around Bristol and its suburbs but usually returned home with faulty brakes, slipping clutches, no windscreen wipers or direction indicators — not to mention tyres in a sorry state. Somehow, we survived.

Another friend Steve, whose father had passed away when he was sixteen, inherited an old Austin Sports car. He spent many years renovating the Austin, which served us well, transporting drunken eighteen-year-old college boys to various parties in Bristol, often in first gear in thick fog, and to the local indoor heated swimming pool which opened in September 1961 in Soundwell, Bristol. A big difference from the cold spring water of the local community centre where we had been taken to learn to swim at the age of eleven upon entrance to Kingswood Grammar School. What an induction! Much shivering and refusal to jump in before PE teacher Jimmy Wilde slapped your backside with a running shoe or dap. Allowed in those days!

My studies had progressed well through 'O' Levels and into the sixth form, for 'A' levels, under the watchful eye of headmaster C.N. Ridley and his staff. He was a remarkable man, who had been a headmaster for almost thirty years, but seemed to be uniformly disliked by staff and pupils. He took the school, for mainly lower middle-class students, to the top of the county table with many university and Oxbridge successes.

Ridley himself came from a working-class background in Sheffield, won a scholarship to Cambridge and taught at Harrow. He supported the house system and prefect system in the school, hated soccer but loved rugby for boys and hockey for girls. Eventually, the soccer lobby overwhelmed him and he was forced towards the end of his stewardship to allow the ruffians' game to be played by school teams. As a prefect I made the occasional visit to the Ridley home and enjoyed his hospitality and more approachable side. No surprise then to learn, forty years later, that the Ridley family had adopted a pupil at Kingswood Grammar School and brought him up as their own. Needless to say, we knew none of this during our school days.

Girlfriends came and went, and young and tender hearts were broken. School dances were infrequent but by early 1963, the so-called Swingin' Sixties arrived with the Beatles and the Rolling Stones. Suddenly, lunchtime music festivals were convened in the school hall, and a few friends actually had record players with a stylus and diamond needles. I didn't, although Dad lent me his school tape recorder to grab music off the huge Bush radio in the living room of our flat. Not long after, I got my first treasured transistor radio. Music now rivalled first team rugby on weekends. I never saw the Beatles live but rode on my friend Martyn's scooter to Longleat on August 2, 1964, to see the Rolling Stones. Great trip, poor audio, and my mother furious that I had travelled on the back of a motorbike.

I sat for my first 'A' levels in June 1963, in French, history and geography. I got reasonable passes but not enough, as a baby boomer, to earn a university place. Dad persuaded me to do a final year to try and improve my grades. Career guidance was almost non-existent in the sixties, so I still had no idea of my future path in life. Anyway, it meant another year in the first rugby XV, so not too bad.

I did not know the world outside family and school, so I was overjoyed to get a first job as a Christmas postman in a Bristol suburb. I delivered parcels from a chartered bus and sorted mail at the main post office. Some of my friends were also there so it was fun, but also somewhat frightening to meet older people who had started their working lives before the war. I saw kindness in them but also a certain hardness of spirit. The toughness did not prevent one of the senior post ladies from trying to seduce me! I suppose she thought I was young and tasty.

During my last nine months at school, I had some pocket money and occasionally went with the daughter of one of my father's friends to the so-called Chinese Jazz Club at the Corn Exchange in Bristol. I relished seeing some of the great American blues singers including John Lee Hooker, Sonny Boy Williamson and

Little Walter. Just around the corner was Carwardines Coffee House, home of the Avon Cities Jazz Band from 1949 to 2000. Stomping jazz, highlighting great musicians who would later play for me when I ran the student dances in Cheltenham from 1965 to 1966.

During the next four years or so after school and during college vacations, I had a number of jobs. These exposed me to interesting but sometimes dangerous persons and outrageous circumstances. Having been a Christmas postie, I was asked by a regular postman to take over his round for several summers as he visited his sister in the USA. Delivering letters to households on a regular beat or walk introduced me to the local moaner who was always complaining about lost mail, undelivered mail containing money, and missing parcels. Easy to shut him up. All I did was to write DOG LOOSE on his mail and refuse to deliver it. I forced him to go to the post office to fetch his own mail. Dogs were and are a real problem for postmen, especially those who wait inside the house for letters to come through the post box and bite the hand pushing in the mail. One such dog waited every day for me, so, I wrapped the mail for this house around a metal file and pushed it through the box. There was a strange howling noise as Rover snapped his teeth on the uncomfortable metal. Needless to say, he was not a problem after that; nor was his owner.

One enjoyable round took me to a rural part of Bristol in the 1960s. Many of the farms were owned by

Quakers who were fine people but reticent to mix with non-believers. However, I had been to primary school with some of their children, so they would always give me a cup of tea and cake, or in the summer cider and a sandwich. I attended the Quakers meeting hall in Frenchay, Bristol from time to time and regretted when the local Quakers sold their farms to the government, who promptly constructed the M4 motorway to Cardiff and London.

I loved hearing the chimes of the ice cream van at the end of my road, especially in summer, and kids seemed to be endlessly buying ice cream. Thinking this must be a good money-making job for me, I answered an advert in the local paper, the Evening Post, to train as an ice cream salesman. I met the fellow who was to train me and reported for duty in Hartcliffe, Bristol on a Sunday morning.

The van had no ice cream on board, so the first job was to buy supplies. To my amazement, we went to a council house on the Hartcliffe council estate, where no one lived, and every room was full of deep freezers full of all types of ice cream. I took my stock for the day, about a hundred pounds' worth, on approval, and loaded the ice cream into the van. Then the fun began as my trainer and I negotiated for places to stop around south Bristol and chime up to attract buyers. Little did I know that many sites or pitches belonged, or so they said, to other ice cream salesmen who resented my presence. They started threatening to beat me up and tried to drive me off the road. Coming from a socialist trade union family, I was surprised with this aspect of worker antipathy and decided that this day would be my first and only try at being an ice cream salesman. Next day I did not go back and left my trainer with a hundred pounds' worth of ice cream unsold.

As a student, I needed to earn money during the summer vacations and eventually, through my father, got a job as a labourer with a building company that specialised in school maintenance. I returned to this job the next couple of summers. The work, not exactly calling on the education of a trainee teacher with three 'A' levels, consisted of breaking up floors, smashing toilet pans, decorating, plumbing, removing tiles, mixing cement, primitive carpentry and demolishing chimneys and walls. My work mates, who ranged from sixteen to sixty plus, were generally nice guys who had endured a hard life on their weekly pay packets. Many were married with children and enjoyed a drink after hours in a pub on their street. There was still a tremendous sense of community in Bristol in the sixties. The younger, unmarried guys drank and ran after girls at the frequent street parties. The company employed one girl as a secretary, deemed the office tart.

Every day, we would pick up our job and time sheets and drive around in a company truck or van to our first site. The company specialised in school repairs, so we usually met the headteacher or caretaker for a briefing. Most clients were usually pleasant and sensible although I can still remember the headteacher who insisted we checked the leaks in the school fuel tanks by opening then with an acetylene torch! My foreman promptly told him the school would be blown sky high and there was no fucking way he would do that! The headmaster was not amused and reported the foreman to the company owner. Nothing happened.

The painting team spent their whole year going from school to school. They were a happy group, a bit like the Ragged Trousered Philanthropists, but among them were two gay guys. In the early 1960s, most gay guys kept their preference to themselves and as a nineteen-year-old straight out of grammar school, I had never knowingly met a homosexual person. Anyway, the straight guys conspired to trap me in a toilet stall with the two gentlemen painters, who approached me and made suggestions. I told them to fuck off and threatened to punch one of them. Suddenly, howls of laughter broke out as the rest of the gang, who had engineered the meeting, emerged from the nearby toilet stalls. The incident was soon forgotten by them, but not by me.

Another day, another job. This time we were not in a school but in a bank at Avonmouth near Bristol. We had been repairing some doors when I spied a good-looking bank clerk. We met on a few occasions, and she was very daring. She once undid my trousers and took out my penis whilst we were out on a park bench. I thought I would be arrested by the police for indecent behaviour.

The owner of the building company did not check on the backgrounds of his employees. Unknown to him, he had employed two recently released prisoners. One of them, call him Jim, was a thief or kleptomaniac. He could not resist stealing something wherever he was. I saw him nab light bulbs, library books, cups, tools, soap — all of which he put into the baskets of his scooter. Harmless guy but professional petty thief.

The second guy, Mike, had just come out of prison after a five-year stretch. He had attacked a postman and stolen the registered letters containing money. I wondered how his National Employment card did not have any gaps on it. After all, he had been away for five years. He said his sister kept up the information on his card when he was inside. Clever guy! As I got to know Mike, I realised he could be violent, but somehow, he liked me. We were employed to destroy some chimneys and old walls at a school site. Our equipment was a power drill and hammer run off a compressor. The noise and vibrations were so horrendous we became temporarily deaf and often had pins and needles and shakes in our arms. Health and safety in 1964? Mike and I got on with the job, and he told me of his deprived life as a youngster. It made me appreciate how lucky I had been so far in my life. Mike would say every day, it's me against them. I can't help it! Eventually, we went to different worksites and we didn't meet again. Maybe Mike ended back in jail for robbery.

As I approached and went past the legal drinking age of eighteen, and had some pocket money, I could enjoy myself in pubs and restaurants without my parents. In the north of England, where I visited my cousins, including the delightful Boris, who had contracted meningitis at age five, I drank scotch and peppermint and Babycham and orange. At this age, I thought beer and wine tasted rotten.

In Bristol, Berni Inns, Britain's first American-style restaurant chain, had opened an outlet in the late fifties as rationing finished. It served a wonderful steak and chips with trimmings for under ten shillings. My mother had never dished up steak, so this was a great treat for a hungry eighteen-year-old in 1963.

Meanwhile in Wales, cousin Richard had turned nineteen and so my thoughts were of a nice boozy evening in a Welsh country pub. His parents had none of it, so we sat outside, Richard and I, and were given lemonade or pop and crisps. Worse came on his twenty-first, when our parents drank all the beer and wine and condemned us to shandy (lemonade and beer) as a concession. Must have been something to do with the Welsh Methodists and temperance.

In March 1964, I found out that the Bristol Royal Infirmary, where I was born in 1945, had demolished the old Georgian maternity house in Southwell Street, Kingsdown. It had been replaced with the present hospital and its landmark chimney. Maybe it was time to think of leaving Bristol. Dad, at age fifty, had just managed to buy his first house in Downend, and so during my last eighteen months at school we left our flat and moved to the almost rustic suburb at the end of a bus route.

In August 1964, I got my 'A' level results and had done no better than last time. I did win a county major scholarship with three 'A' levels, but no university place. Career guidance at school was poor. I had no idea of what I wanted to do for the rest of my life. Dad intervened and suggested teacher training college at St. Paul's Cheltenham, where he had been a student from 1931 to 33. I got a place and started at St. Paul's in September 1964. Unknown to me, Dad's stepmother Ida was still alive and she, the Tailor of Gloucester's second wife, lived nearby in Charlton Kings. My life and ancestors were coming together.

My father had retained little contact with Ida, his stepmother, who became the second wife of John Samuel Prichard, the so-called Tailor of Gloucester, as personified in Beatrix Potter's book published in 1903. Prichard had married my grandmother, Martha Ellen Williams in Newent in Gloucestershire in 1907, when she was seventeen. By 1913 they had produced four children: Cristobel, Leslie, Enid and my father, Adrian John Prichard. Martha was a strong character even then, and her father was against the marriage but gave her as a wedding present the money she could have expected on his death.

John Prichard was more than ten years older than Martha Ellen, and family gossip says the marriage was turbulent. Dad was born in the village of Hardwicke, near Gloucester in 1913, the youngest of the children from John and Martha's marriage. He was a sickly child and according to his sister Enid, who lived until the age of ninety-three, spent the first six months lying on a cushion, as his infant tummy was so sensitive. Probably explains the reason for his windy disposition throughout his life!

Eventually, Martha Ellen was accused of adultery by John Prichard. She said he attacked her violently, and she ran away, probably in 1914, with the two youngest children, Adrian and Enid. Left behind were Cristobel and Leslie. John Prichard had a housekeeper called Ida Powell, at the time, and like so many single or deserted men, he crossed the landing and married Ida in 1917. They produced a half-brother for the other children, called Douglas, whom I never met. Martha Ellen ran away to the north of England, and settled near Bolton, working at various occupations including owning a shop, becoming the mayor of her town and being a lifelong socialist who hoarded tinned food in her pantry.

John Prichard died in 1934, from consumption. He coughed himself to death in his garden shed. Martha Ellen died in 1958 of a botched gallbladder operation. By then she was known as Martha Ellen Welch, having met and apparently married the man I called Grandad, Joseph Edwin Welch, a first world war survivor and lifelong devotee of alcohol.

About to go to St. Paul's College, Cheltenham in 1931, my father needed a birth certificate. No doubt the marriage breakup many years before led to the loss of his original certificate. Dad was already calling himself Adrian Welch, and so he managed to get a new certificate in that name. Prichard was a phantom of the past, but legally he was still a Prichard. This legacy haunted him for the rest of his life, and few people knew his secret. Eventually, when he died, he left me a note explaining the situation, and a friendly registrar accepted his will in the name of Welch. In France, where I am writing this book, the 'cas judiciare' would have gone on for years!

When Dad went up to college in 1931, John Prichard was still alive, finally passing away in 1934. My father told me that he once visited his father, but after maybe sixteen years of little contact, he felt there was little between them, and Ida was not very friendly.

Growing up, there were occasional visits to and from Dad's sister Cristobel, known as Chrissie, and his brother Leslie. Both suffered bouts of insecurity and depression throughout their lives, and for many years I was unsure as to their real identities. Auntie Enid, a real jewel, died a lifelong socialist aged ninety-three, in 2010. Her funeral music was 'My Way' and 'The Red

Flag', with a humanist service. No bloody church for her!

So in late September 1964, it seemed strange that I was taken to meet Aunt Ida, in Charlton Kings, near Cheltenham. Maybe Dad wanted to show off his son, who was going up to the teacher training college. Ida lived in a pretty cottage, not far from the church. An old lady, with seven months to live, white hair and stooped, no good emotions emanated from her. She had not treated Leslie and Cristobel well and had preferred her only son Douglas. Even he had problems with her, when she took an instant dislike to his wife to be, and the potential bride vowed never to visit her again. That's just what happened! I was never to see Ida again; she died in 1965 aged seventy-five, and her ashes were buried alongside John Samuel Prichard.

St. Paul's Teacher Training College or College of Education, Cheltenham, in September 1964, was an eclectic mix of nineteen-year-old former schoolboys from grammar, early comprehensive and public schools, and foreign mature students from industry, the armed forces and the liberal professions. No ladies — they were up the road at St. Mary's College of Education.

The war had been over for twenty years, and education had been being expanded at a fast pace, demanding teachers and lecturers. Former schoolboys like me, mature students, were encouraged to come into the profession of teaching, offering their maturity and experience of life to the classroom. One fellow, a former major in the army, had driven back from his last posting in Kenya. He had all sorts of animal horns and paraphernalia attached to his radiator and bonnet. We called him Bwana Bowles! Another drove an ancient VW Beetle from Germany and sounded a bit Germanic. Don't know what side of the war he had been on!

My first two years were spent in a college hostel called Rosehill, on a very pleasant site near the present-day Cheltenham Racecourse. Needless to say, the students, including me, wrote rude words in big letters on the racetrack during the Cheltenham Festival Week in March each year. Each student at Rosehill had his own room, and cleaners who looked after every room. I guess we were spoilt. Most of the rooms had a view of the trees and fields around the hockey pitch, and the large bent tree next to it. I will come back to the tree later on!

The Rosehill site was glorious in summer, and girlfriends were allowed into our rooms until nine p.m. at weekends. At least that was supposed to be the rule. The bursar at the time reputedly used to walk by the rooms on sunny Saturday afternoons, see all the curtains drawn, and say, "The lads are at it today!" Occasionally for legal reasons, and perhaps moral ones as well, a fire drill bell would shriek away, and we would all have to leave our rooms and assemble on the field past midnight. Some guys would refuse to come out of their rooms, pretending they had suddenly gone deaf.

Occasionally a sheepish looking girl would appear to a roar of approval from the guys assembled on the field.

This was my first experience of living in a dormitory or hostel with a group of fellows who had been randomly put together. There was the son of an aristocrat, the eldest son of a famous headmaster, a vicar's son, a teacher's son like me, a mature student from Burma and a West Indian called Trevor T., who had been living in the UK for some time.

The fellow from Burma constantly munched on nuts, explaining to me that they enhanced his sexuality. Trevor T. was the second black person with whom I had ever become friends. Between 1956 and 1964, only two black pupils had attended my grammar school. Trevor had come to live in Bristol as a young man and had decided to go into teaching at about age thirty. He was well dressed and regarded the black students from Africa as well below him. So much so, that when I introduced him to a black student from Cameroon, and suggested they have a drink together, he protested and snapped, "Do you really want me to go out with this bloody *** from the jungle?" I could not believe it. Never heard anything like it before. But that was Trevor!

We all ate together in the big house attached to the hostels. The food was good; we never heard of any vegetarians in those days. The guys had plenty of serving wenches to ogle, and every Thursday at seven thirty p.m. we all assembled in front of the TV, not widescreen in those days, to watch 'Top of the Pops'. The legendary show started on January 1, 1964, and lasted forty-two years until July 30, 2006. It gave us an intoxicating dose of popular culture, for baby boomers or mature students.

Students destined for teaching in those days went through a few weeks of orientation at college, and then we were pushed out for a month into primary schools around Cheltenham to see if we had any potential teaching ability. I was sent to an old, dilapidated primary school in Stroud, Gloucestershire. October 1964 was a beautiful month, a real Indian summer. The sun shone every day, but I learnt very little about becoming a teacher. From schoolboy to schoolteacher in six months was too much. Anyway, I passed the statutory test and returned to college to begin the academic side of the course. My main subjects were French and history, with a whole host of other subjects, such as physical education, education, divinity, health education and English. All these subjects were designed to equip me to have a broad base of teaching ability in the classroom.

The French department was headed by Mr Bertram Winkless, a kind old man, with bespectacled, grey hair and a baggy suit — very knowledgeable, but mentally and perhaps physically damaged after several years in a Japanese prisoner-of-war camp during World War II. Cruelly, we would play upon his short temper, when he asked questions like what is your philosophy of life?

Philosophy of life, at nineteen? I responded, beer, women and money! He would go ballistic and scream about how he had endured terrible hardships in the war and had to endure garbage like that.

I came from a family with connections in France and had even visited it before college. But on the whole, my poor level of spoken French drove Winkless or Winkie, as we nicknamed him, completely mad. He once asked Mick G. what he liked to eat in France. Mick G. was a PE lad doing French as second subject, so he said in his loud north-country voice, with a terrible French accent, "Je veux a bloody jambon butty!" The class collapsed. Winkie thought he was taking the piss out of him and became even more demonic! I think Mick eventually passed French — God knows how.

The college in the beautiful town of Cheltenham was men only, with the women's college close by. Some students were obviously very sexually active, but some of the guys had come from minor public schools where girl pupils had never been admitted. One such fellow, William, approached me once, and asked how he should show a girl he fancied her. So, maliciously, I explained to him, girls' breasts were very sensitive and that was the way he should first show his interest. So, at the next college dance, he danced with his chosen one and immediately started touching her tits. There was a scream from the dance floor and William staggered backwards, pursued by a girl shouting, "You fucking pervert!" It was 1964 after all. William came to see me

— most hurt. So, I explained to him that he needed more practice and should try again.

Some guys always seemed to be piggish with their food. One fellow from Birmingham, Roger, would eat too much, particularly in the evenings. A few of us spotted this habit and noticed that after supper he would run to his room to vomit in the washbasin. One evening, before supper, we took the pipe off the bottom of his washbasin! We watched Roger stuffing himself and quickly followed him to his room. He ran the tap and started vomiting, but let out a howl of disbelief as cold water and vomit ran over his shoes! That cured him for a while.

In the same block as Roger lived a fellow from Stoke-on-Trent called Harry. This gentleman was a fearless amateur fire-eater. Harry decided to give an exhibition one late spring afternoon, and not being professional, blew into the wind. The flames shot back at his face and seared him, amid much screaming and swearing! Harry ended up in hospital and gave up fire-eating. Funny how teachers always want to make an exhibition of themselves.

Maurice Pick was the head of history. A charming man who believed in visiting historical sites with students. My first memorable visit was to the Cistercian abbey of Tintern, in Gwent, South Wales. Apparently, the monks drank cider from apples grown nearby. I certainly indulged in some cider that day and remember plying Maurice Pick with questions about monks, nuns, drinking and so on. He seemed bemused but no doubt realised I was pissed. Year one studies continued successfully although not very challengingly. Preparation for life as a teacher was far too academic, offering little practical information on how to teach.

On the social side I met my first serious girlfriend since school: a blonde Welsh girl from Cardiff called Ruth, a student at St. Mary's College of Education. We went out for most of college first year; I visited her home and she came to mine. But somehow, I messed it up and we split up. I was broken-hearted!

At the same time, I attended the college functions and dances in the strangely named Shaftesbury Hall. I put myself up for election as social secretary and got elected. I become responsible for booking the bands or acts for the Saturday functions. It was the middle sixties. The Beatles and The Rolling Stones were big, and there were many bands from the UK and USA regularly touring UK campuses. Brian Epstein, powerful manager of the Beatles, collaborated for a period with Robert Stigwood, later to manage the Bee Gees. I received correspondence from both of them about the bands they represented. What a time!

I put shows on cheaply, usually for no more than two hundred and fifty pounds. I booked some of the great names of pop: Stevie Winwood of the Spencer Davis Group, Brian Auger and Julie Driscoll of Steam Packet, Long John Baldry, Billy J. Kramer, Jimmy Winston of the Small Faces, Graham Bond, Jack Bruce and Ginger Baker of Cream, the Fortunes, the Ramrods from Cheltenham, and an outrageous American singer called Sugar Pie Dessanto, who lifted her skirts in front of me.

All of the acts were booked through a snazzy guy called Mike Lloyd from Stoke-on-Trent. Mike impressed penniless students like me with his sports car and dinners at Cheltenham's leading restaurants. Mike worked for the strangely named Terry Blood Agency and travelled to campuses across the UK, booking bands for functions. I thought of doing this for a living instead of teaching. Ambitiously entrepreneurial, Mike was to eventually set up the Mike Lloyd record shops in Stoke-on-Trent. Not heard from him since the sixties.

The office of social secretary was a fount for girlfriends that year, not to mention having dinner with the principal of St. Mary's College of Education. Her niece was visiting her, and I had to take this rather plain and reticent girl to the Saturday function. I felt like introducing her to William to see if she would come to life if he tickled her heart. Needless to say, the young lady returned untouched to her aunt.

St. Paul's College of Education was firmly rooted in Church of England beliefs. It had its own magnificent chapel and at that time a chaplain called Rev G.I.F. Thomson — GIFT for short. Indeed, he was a gift, always chattering on in his mellifluous voice. He was destined for great things in the church, but had obviously upset someone in the hierarchy and been banished to Cheltenham.

Each student was supposed to attend chapel at least once a week. I had been confirmed at age sixteen, but after my godfather had threatened to kick the fucking bishop over the ownership of his farm, I had rather abandoned the church. Every Sunday morning after an evening of debauchery and drinking, too early for me to rise, a column of sinner cyclists left the hostel for chapel. Eventually, succumbing to pressure, I made a visit to chapel one Sunday morning, but after five minutes, blood began pouring out of my nose, and I had to be helped out. God had sent me a message not to come into his house, so I never went back until 2016.

Illness at college meant, if you were lucky, a stay in the sanatorium or sick room. Rugby injuries and tonsilitis gave me several sojourns in the san. It usually meant Matron clucking all over you and occasional visits from a local doctor and every evening the principal. He can best be described as an avuncular Christian who lived for his job. Always asking pertinent questions as to our wellbeing and trying to ensure we were not slacking. Matron was certainly no beauty, but we dared each other to pull back our blankets and show her an erection. She would have died. Sorry we never did!

Parents' visits to college were always a good time. Mum would bring cakes and fresh clothes, although by then I had a girlfriend who helped with ironing shirts.

One slept on underpants and socks under the bed to make them flat. On one of my parents' visits we went to see Aunt Chrissie, or Cristobel, the Tailor of Gloucester's eldest daughter. She lived in Stroud and was married to Mr John Butcher, a local businessman. One of his businesses was the importation of golf balls from the USA. Butcher was friendly with the author, poet and novelist Laurie Lee, most famous for his book 'Cider with Rosie'. He lived in nearby Slad. I remember meeting a kindly, obviously sensitive man who talked niceties with a twenty-year-old. I was to see him again in the 1970s, changing trains at Reading station. Always wished I had more time to speak to such a wonderful writer. Later, I was to compare him to the evocative French writer, Jean Giono, who wrote so sympathetically about his native Provence and nature. Giono, who was alive in the 1960s, had the decency to respond to letters from French students in the Cotswolds.

French and history student I was, but I could also play a good game of rugby. St. Paul's College had a tradition of producing PE and games teachers, and of course had a great rugby team. I was fortunate enough to play for the First XV on about twenty occasions, even though I was regarded as something of a misfit, not being a PE student.

The standard of rugby was very high and many of the players played international or top provincial rugby. Rugby attracted many good-looking girls. I also enjoyed piss-ups and occasional brawls on, as well as off, the pitch. I can vaguely remember smashing up the Angel Hotel in Cardiff and a few bars in Cheltenham. Visits to the Oxford colleges and various forces bases showed the other side of life to a team of lower middle-class thugs. A visit to the army officers' training base at Shrivenham in Oxfordshire was a highlight as we had batmen serving us with pints of ale as we came off the pitch and foaming baths nearby in the officers' changing rooms. The enjoyment must have persuaded some of the college players to take up careers in the armed forces. Years to come, alumni lists showed former students on army bases throughout the world. There were no drugs then; at least I was not aware of them. I made do with college grub, and training twice a week which usually consisted of a run and a few passing movements. Nothing like I was to find in France eighteen months later.

At this stage in my life, I did not have a car but would occasionally hire one illegally from a fellow student who was an England water polo player. One night I set off on a high-speed drive to Hereford, certainly uninsured, to visit a girlfriend now resident at the local college of education. There must have been much squealing of tyres and skidding, but fortunately there were no police around. The visit was successful and somehow, I returned safely that night.

My friend Stephen W. had accompanied me to college from school; indeed my father had driven us both to college in September 1964. Steve's dad had passed away some years before, and Steve had inherited an old off-white Austin Seven Sports car circa 1934. We all helped him to lovingly restore it during our sixth form days.

Steve eventually drove the car to Cheltenham and kept it at college for weekends. One weekend, after much alcohol, Steve decided to drive me back to the hostel. It was a foggy night, and we decided to drive across the grass in front of my building, forgetting the small tree in the middle of the field that we suddenly crashed into. The tree bent, and the car lurched up the trunk into the branches. We must have banged our heads on the windscreen and passed out. Upon waking up, I said to Steve, as the car rocked gently, are we in heaven? No, he said, we're in the fucking tree. Steam poured from the bonnet and the engine was making a staccato noise. The exhaust pipe had folded like a concertina!

Somehow, we managed to pull the car off the tree and abandon it on the hostel driveway for the night. Can't remember what we told the warden next day! Lack of a regular car meant that girlfriends from out of town had to thumb lifts from passing motorists. One of my friends, Jan, got a lift one night from a creepy fellow who made suggestions to her. She complained to me about this, so the next time we were due to meet, I thumbed a lift to her college in Gloucester. We had a great evening at a college function, and she accompanied me to the usual place for thumbing lifts. A guy pulled up in a grey van and asked where I was going. Cheltenham, I said. He told me to get in, and halfway to Cheltenham, he started trying to fondle me and put his hands on my legs. I threatened to give him the biggest thrashing of his life if he touched me again. Eventually I got out and told him to piss off. I never forgot his face, and only years later did I realise it was Fred West, the serial murderer. Jan later told me that she saw the guy who picked me up, and it was the same guy who had made suggestions to her.

My second teaching practice in spring 1966 was in Birmingham, at a comprehensive school. I witnessed some of the worst teaching I had ever seen. Many of the teachers ruled the children by fear. They regularly punched and kicked. Most learning involved copying passages from the board and keeping quiet, or else. Impossible to try out some of the new teaching ideas of the time as the kids took this as a sign of weakness and would try and play the fool. I didn't enjoy this teaching practice and luckily got tonsilitis, and so spent one week with Matron in the sanatorium back in Cheltenham.

Another school visit to a very progressive primary school about fifty miles from Cheltenham was more profitable and enjoyable. In the school, self-motivated children worked all day, almost without teacher guidance. I was twenty years of age and spotted a buxom lady teacher dressed in red. She had great legs as well. We got talking and I arranged to miss the bus to college and take her for dinner in the village. She was a flautist, but that night she played something else. Next morning, I thumbed a lift back to Cheltenham with a broad grin on my face.

Two years at college had soon passed by, and I was selected to do one year in France, as a language assistant at a French lycée. I asked to be sent to the south of France, preferably to a town with a good rugby team! Before that in summer 1966, I had worked as a builder's labourer to finance the trip to France. Painting schools, refurbishing toilets, fitting new doors and cupboards and the tedious job of preparing floors for concrete: these were some of my daily duties. Made me glad I was going to college and not stuck as a labourer for life.

My co-workers were a cunning lot. They knew every trick in the book to gain a little time, work less, claim overtime, and generally cheat the owners of the company. Unfortunately, the owner was a friend of my father's and my colleagues knew this. I needed to keep my mouth shut and work like them. This was the mid-sixties, and these fellows had a strong street or community sense. There was much talk about their local pub and street parties.

One of the labourers, Raymond, always came to work in his suit with collar and tie before changing into his overalls. Raymond spent most evenings in his local pub in Bedminster, Bristol. He was a strong man, even in his sixties and along with Vic, the carpenter had a great collection of jokes.

The only young man was another Raymond, or Ray for short, who was an apprentice plumber. He was learning the trade from a pair of veterans, Jim and Lloyd. They made Ray do the dirtiest jobs, like cleaning the toilet basins to be replaced. He worried constantly that he had got at least one of his girlfriends pregnant, and might have to buy a pram and cot. Ray once confided to me that his parents took no interest in his career or life, so he did what he wanted. I realised how lucky I was that my parents cared about my future.

During the rest of summer 1966, I caught up with a few old girlfriends in Bristol and on July 5, 1966, celebrated my twenty-first birthday with my parents and a few friends at home. Nothing like the bashes they have these days. Also I made my last trip on the Aust ferry, across the Severn Estuary, separating England from Wales. This old boat service saved the motorist from Bristol about fifty miles on a trip to Wales. The ferry closed in September 1966 as the motorway system and new bridge encroached upon Bristol.

After working for about ten weeks, I had saved enough money to book my plane ticket to south west France with a little spending money remaining. I was going to fly to Pau and then get a taxi to Oloron-Sainte-Marie, a small town at the foot of the Pyrenees. Here I would be an assistant or English language teacher at the local lycée. There was only one other English person living in Oloron at this time. I had to survive, perfect my

French and accept this life-changing opportunity. And oh boy, what an opportunity!

I came out of the airport at Pau with two cases and an immediate feeling I was going to like this region with its vivid colours, distant mountains and sunburnt girls. This was the end of September 1966, and the late afternoon heat was immense. I found a taxi and told the driver to take me to Oloron, about sixty kilometres away. Said I wanted a good hotel in the town. Very hard to book this far ahead in those days! Eventually we pulled up outside the Hotel de la Poste. Every French town seems to have an Hotel de la Poste or an Hotel Bristol! The owner had a room available for two nights. I took the room knowing that I only had enough money to cover the stay. I came down for dinner and looked at the menu. Unbelievable! Sheep's brains and tripe. I had never eaten that stuff before. Certainly not food for a starving Englishman. I managed to get the owner/chef to do me a steak and chips. Even that was difficult: the steak was still too bloody rare for me!

Next morning, I had croissants and coffee and went to see a teacher from the school who had been put in touch with me. She lent me a bike, so I cycled to one of the banks in town where I knew the manager to be the secretary of the rugby club. He knew who I was, helped me to open a bank account, and gave me directions to the rugby club, and a few addresses where I might be able to rent a room. I spent the rest of the day cycling around Oloron with its gave or river, gaily painted homes and shops, cathedral and chocolate and beret factories. In the background were the magical Pyrenees mountains, separating France and Spain. What a beautiful place to spend the next year!

After another difficult culinary experience at the Hotel de la Poste, I managed to find lodgings with a couple in a modern house on the outskirts of Oloron. Not too far from the school and rugby club, but also close to the chocolate factory, which emitted a wonderful smell at all times. My landlords worked in the local Basque beret factory and in the evenings, I looked at French TV with them. My French comprehension sped up very quickly. Totally immersed in French and with only one other English person in town, who I saw rarely, my brain took a battering. By the evening I was exhausted and longed to speak English, but even visiting a bar for a drink meant more French.

I put my priorities first and found the local rugby club, FC Oloron, then one of the top sixty-four clubs in France! They were expecting me, this young Englishman who would be only one of two English guys playing in France in 1966/67. I got my rugby licence, no such thing in England at that time, and swore that I had never played rugby league or treize as they called it. Big crime in those days.

The president of the club owned the local panel-beating garage and the secretary owned the best bar restaurant. You can guess where all the club dinners and lunches after Wednesday training happened. Perfect setup. We trained on Wednesdays at lunchtime and on Thursdays in the evenings. Games were played on Sundays. Shamateurism was rife, and all the first team players, including me, received an envelope stuffed full of francs. At that time, Oloron had two recent internationals in Saux and Abadie and were light years ahead of English teams in terms of training and movement on the pitch. The municipal stadium regularly attracted five thousand spectators for the top games. But first I had to get fit and train in the end of summer heat with the noise of the crickets and frogs all around me. And so, to the lycée, where I was going to work as an English language assistant.

The lycée was brand new and right next to the rugby stadium. I wanted to have a room in the school boarding block along with the 'peons', or university students who looked after the pupils in residence. For some reason it was not allowed, but I managed to nab a room where I could have my afternoon nap or siesta. I taught in the mornings and late afternoons. School lunch was amazing, and they even served wine to us. The minister of agriculture was a wine grower until he was replaced by the new minister of agriculture, a dairy farmer, and milk replaced the wine. We had a student revolt and lunch tables were overturned.

After lunch the 'peons', now my friends, took me to a local café, where we had brandy and coffee and the boys ogled the girls. Brandy and coffee of course meant a siesta in the afternoon before I returned to my teaching duties of about twelve hours a week. The pupils tried hard to speak English, and many of them were just two years younger than me, including some good-looking girls. I remember trying to plug in the projector whilst looking at a great pair of legs, and accidentally shocking myself. My hair stood on end, and the pupils fell about laughing.

It was wonderful to meet young French men and women in their own country. Remember in the mid-sixties, meeting French citizens in the UK was rare. Some of the guys were Pieds-Noirs, or Frenchmen born in Algeria, who in 1960, after the revolutionary war, had been repatriated in France. They still had deep regrets and were regarded with suspicion by the locals. At that time as well, the Basque separatists were at work in the region, and I met some who had been tortured by the Spanish police. I made a good friend in Pancho Daguerre, an ardent Basque-speaking separatist. Despite a damaged leg from birth, he was a great pelote basque player, and taught me the rudiments of the game. We survived a drunken car crash together, as did our girlfriends in the back. The crash followed a thrilling pursuit from another driver we had pushed off the road. Somehow, we drove home in our wrecked Renault Dauphine which looked like a squashed accordion.

Summer seemed to last forever in 1966, as the weather in south west France continued to be warm, and the insects crashed into the floodlights during night training sessions. We played rugby in many towns across southern France: Biarritz, Orthez, Bayonne, Pau, Mont de Marsan, Dax, Lourdes. This was the real heartland of French rugby, and I met many legendary players including the Boniface brothers, who drove pink Rolls Royces, and the young Robert Paparemborde.

Some games were very rough, and on one post-game occasion, we had to be escorted by the police to our bus! But usually, as Andre Herrero, a former French captain and trainer, said to me years later, we all finished with wine, pâté and a look at the local girls with their enticing olive skins. During the autumn of 1966, the early months of my stay in France, I went out with a few local girls, but then I met Marie Therese, or Maite, who was a stunning Basque girl. Dark hair, almond shaped face, olive complexion, black eyes and a great body. I was smitten as I had never seen girls like this before, except in the movies. We were attracted to each other. Marie Therese was to be part of my life for a long time.

France had its own pop music stars at the time: Francoise Hardy, Joe Dassin, Johnny Hallyday, to name a few. But this was the time of the Beatles invasion, and so it was hip to be British in Oloron-Sainte-Marie. And I was the only British male in the town. Later in May 1967, perhaps the biggest record of the period hit the French airways: A Whiter Shade of Pale, by Procol Harum. Even the French hummed this one, and every time I hear it now, it still reminds me of the good times in France in 1966/67.

Back home in Britain, the Wilson government was in power and I remember French state television, ORTF, at the time regularly painting a very grey picture of the UK. De Gaulle was still in power, and at a political rally his henchmen looked ominous and his dislike of the English after his wartime experience might explain the hostility. Nevertheless, France seemed to be economically ahead of the UK at this time. New roads, public buildings, schools and day-to-day life seemed more agreeable. Indeed, I was taking a siesta one afternoon in my little room in the new school dormitory when I was awoken by an explosion. No, there were no girls involved! The ceiling collapsed on top of me, and the room got clogged with dust! For a moment I thought there had been an earthquake! Soon my colleagues ran down the corridor to pull me out and explain that Concorde had flown overhead from Toulouse and done a supersonic test! Obviously, no rules about tests over inhabited areas existed in those days! Later on, I endured several proper earthquakes in Oloron and in the heart of the Basque region at Saint Jean Pied de Port, a sweet border town between France and Spain. I was in a farmhouse at the time and the building shook, the bed moved, plaster fell from the walls and it sounded as though a huge lorry was rumbling down the hill outside. The earth really did move for me that time.

My French life continued with Maite, rugby and my French landlords. I rented a room in their home, and they did my washing, but I ate out every night at the local rugby restaurant. My landlords watched TV every night and sometimes invited me to watch with them. Their comments were hilarious during 'Intervilles' and 'Jeux Sans Frontieres', formats that would eventually make it to the UK. And of course, there were the movies from the great French producers/directors of the time like Truffaut, and the town cinema had a club to discuss the movies we had seen. Enlightening for the boy from Bristol.

My parents decided to visit me from Bristol during Easter 1967. They set off in their Vauxhall Viva, crossed the channel and made it in three days. There were not many motorways in France at that time and B routes were not like today. My parents were overwhelmed by the variety and taste of the food in the various hotels and restaurants they sampled. Dad could not work out how to eat artichokes and said he did not want to eat any more bloody thistles. They were making his tongue sore! Maite and I took them to San Sebastian in Spain, which even then under Franco was a stunningly organised place. However, the Spaniards seemed less joyful than the French at this time. In the hotel, we met Willie Hamilton, the socialist anti-royalist MP, from Scotland. Dad, being a strong socialist, struck up a friendship with Hamilton, and they spent the night talking about the Queen Mother's pension and a few other injustices. My mother looked on, talking wisely with Mrs Hamilton, who seemed fed up with the whole thing!

In the morning, we went for a walk along the beach at San Sebastian. I wore shorts although I had been warned the Spanish police did not like shorts or bikinis, so I sensed they were eyeing Maite and I, looking for breaches of Franco's right-wing rules. Later, we set off back for Oloron-Sainte-Marie in the Vauxhall Viva and safely navigated a massive Pyrenean hailstorm. Mum and Dad left for Bristol.

Just one term left for me at the lycée in Oloron-Sainte-Marie, and the summer weather had returned. Maite was working at the University in Pau, and I took my students through to their final classes in English conversation. Most of them seemed better at Spanish than English. Not surprising as the Spanish border was only twenty kilometres away!

I stayed on for the summer of 1967 and enjoyed trips all over the Basque region, sampling more of its wine and food. Maite also organised a trip to the Costa Brava in Spain, with three of her girlfriends. This was 1967 and Salou, the resort, was just being built. Not too many Brits visited at that time. We found an apartment, me and three girls, and lived on roast lamb and red wine. And got very sunburnt. It was not long before the parents of the other girls, and one boyfriend, turned up to check us out. Nothing to report here. The boyfriend then drove us hair-raisingly across the Pyrenees to

Oloron. I remember some dusty Spanish towns, one called Jaca, where we stopped for ham sandwiches and red wine.

Besides visiting the region, I set about training to get fit for the rugby season. I would be returning to St. Paul's College, Cheltenham in September 1967. My girlfriend Maite wanted to join me in the UK, so my dad managed to get her a job as an English assistant in Bristol. She stayed with my parents, which was not a good move. She started to dislike my mother fairly quickly! An omen!

I planned to resume my studies in Cheltenham. Luckily for me, my grandmother bought me her boyfriend's car. The gentleman in question, Mr Maurice French, a former bus inspector, had decided to stop driving. He had a reconditioned 1948 Morris 8, which cost granny twenty — yes, twenty pounds! So, I got my first wheels at age twenty-two, the same age as the car granny had given to me.

I used the car to shuttle between Bristol and Cheltenham and for occasional trips to see my godfather, Uncle Ted, on his farm near Gloucester. He was supposed to leave me the farm in his will, but died intestate, so I was still penniless.

Rugby, Maite and studies took up all my time from September 1967 through June 1968. I needed my teacher's certificate, which guaranteed me a place in educational society. I had to finish studies in French and education, and at the same time the possibilities of a degree in education emerged. The UK government wanted to upgrade the standard of the college of education. To do additional courses in education I was required to indicate my ability: not only to finish my certificate, but deal with the additional workload. I badly wanted to do a Bachelor of Education degree, feeling cheated that I had not been accepted by a university upon leaving grammar school. Dad and Maite encouraged me, so I studied hard. The year went very quickly and finished with a six-week teaching practice in a primary school in rural Warwickshire.

The school was in a village called Lower Quinton, not far from Shipston-on-Stour. The headmaster, Major Styler, retained his title even twenty-three years after the war! I lodged during the week with him and his wife. The college bus dropped me on a Sunday evening at their home in Shipston and I travelled daily with them to the school. I taught a class of ten and eleven-year olds in the school hall because of the lack of space.

The headmaster warned me, but I did not believe him, that the village was blighted with incest and lunacy. Too much inter-breeding, he said! Strangely, during full moon periods, some of the pupils behaved in a bizarre manner and could not concentrate. Maybe the headmaster was right. Anyway, the teaching practice went well, and my reports from my tutor Bob Trafford, who really liked working in and visiting rural schools, were good.

The highlight for me was not the school, but the European Cup Final on May 29, 1968, that ended with the score Manchester United 4 – Benefica 1. The first time an English club had won the prestigious trophy. I watched the game with Major Styler, at his home in Shipston-on-Stour, and dropped into a local pub for a celebratory drink afterwards. What an evening!

The academic year of 1968 soon came to a close. I was delighted to receive my teaching certificate and be selected for the Bachelor of Education degree course in French. The only student left on the course, I would have to face three lecturers alone.

In the summer of 1968, I worked as a relief postman at Fishponds Post Office. I was friendly with our regular deliverer's son, whose family wanted to visit a relation in America. I took over the walk, as they called it, for about six weeks. Early morning starts, but finished by one p.m. A lot of cycling, the occasional savage dog, and in my case, I was continually pursued by a randy post lady! Interesting also to see British trade unionism in action; posties did everything to get round their walk as quickly as possible. Plenty of not at home cards, and parcels stuffed in lockers for later delivery. At least breakfast was good: there were plenty of cakes and sausage rolls from the shop next to the post office.

I noticed changes to Bristol, including the introduction of parking meter maids in June 1967. In Kingswood, there were rumours that the ten pin bowling alley was to close, and it did in November 1968.

Another stop-off site from school had gone! At home my dad was now well into the headship of his last school in St. George, Bristol. And mum still only had a spin dryer, and did all the washing by hand.

By the end of August 1968, I had saved a few pounds in anticipation of my last year at college and marriage to Maite in mid-1969. Back to Cheltenham in September 1968, in my Morris 8, for what turned out to be an exhausting academic year. This was the first year of B.Ed., and everybody wanted the course to stand up to rigorous academic standards for both staff and students. Eventual degrees were to be awarded by Bristol University.

The course in education made us really think about what happened in schools, far more so than the Certificate in Education, which I had just completed. The French course was vast and as the only student, I could not escape if assignments were not complete. The head of department, Mr Winkless, still lapsed into strange moods when he thought of his internment in a Japanese war camp. Kay, the only lady in the department, was only five years older than me and distracted me deeply when she decided to go braless to work. Sometimes I did not know where to look.

I was unable to live in college accommodation during my last two years, and so I secured a room with old-age pensioners in a nearby terraced street. The unheated rooms were ice-cold in winter, and the window panes regularly froze on the inside from my breath. Girls were not allowed in the house, and the landlady carried out regular searches. The fire in the sitting room usually died by nine p.m. so I found warmth by studying back in the warm college library.

Harry and Nel, my landlord and his wife, insisted on making sure we were back by eleven p.m. every evening. By then, Nel was usually asleep in the parlour chair, and Harry had taken out his hearing aid. He would then say, "Goodnight, Rob and John!"

Sure he could not hear, we replied, "Fuck off Harry."

He answered, "Thank you!" It never failed and we would then collapse into bed, wondering if one day his lip reading would improve.

The Bachelor of Education course involved many theoretical educational strands but no teaching practice, and the French course was full of literature and language. All the stuff you really need to be a good teacher.

The workload, playing rugby and seeing my girlfriend Maite, who was still staying with my parents in Bristol, meant that I was fully committed for the academic year September 1968 through June 1969. The old Morris 8 made many return trips between Bristol and Cheltenham without breaking down once. Not bad for a car that was about twenty-three years old.

Eventually, May 1969 arrived and the climax of my final year of study. Two solid weeks of exams. I prepared well, and with the help of study drugs from

Boots the chemist, bombed through two weeks without sleeping. What a relief when it was over.

Maite and I had planned to get married in the summer of 1969, and this we did after my usual temp stint at the post office. We married on July 21, 1969, just as Apollo landed on the moon. Must have been an omen here in a little town in south west France. Parents and family attended, and after the wedding banquet, we set off for our honeymoon in St. Jean de Luz. Disaster struck when the car broke down, and we ended up hitching a lift to the seaside hotel.

During the rest of the holiday in France I learnt that I had passed at Bristol University and had been given a teaching post from September 1969, at Eastville Junior School, in Bristol. The salary was to be nine hundred and eighty pounds per annum. I thought it was a fortune at the time. My bride and I returned to the UK in August 1969, and Maite took up a position at Lloyds Bank in Bristol. We also found lodgings in half of a bungalow in Hanham, on the Bath side of the city. The bungalow owners owned a Dalmatian dog, who spent more time with us than with the owners. Our married life began in three rooms with a borrowed Dalmatian dog, whose mood was variable.

Every day, I commuted from Hanham to central Bristol and back to Eastville. Not too bad in those days, but impossible now. The old Morris 8 began to have mechanical problems. The seats collapsed and had to be put back together with wire. I made the decision to give the Morris 8 to a teacher at my father's school who needed it for spares. I bought a second-hand Hillman Imp. Nice car but endless problems as I was about to find out.

School at Eastville Primary was a revelation to me, and the first time I came into contact with large numbers of black people. When I left Kingswood Grammar School in June 1964, there had been only two black pupils out of nearly nine hundred students. I've told the story of Mike Robinson, a close friend. Only many years later did I realise he was black; his race just never occurred to me.

My parents' open attitude to all folks regardless of colour and race must be congratulated for my openness. Earlier in my life I had had a girlfriend from Ceylon, and a very dark African friend from Mali whose wife was equally black. More of that later.

By now Eastville Primary School was about seventy per cent black and Asiatic, and new pupils were arriving in England over the weekend and coming to register on the Monday. I took the children swimming on a Thursday morning, and one Indian girl jumped in fully clothed, having no idea how to swim. I had to pull her out of the water. She had only been in England for five days!

Eastville School, besides its racial mixture, programmed a class for the deaf and a special class for children with behavioural and learning problems. On reflection, the school was trying to fulfil too many objectives, and was based in a growingly impoverished area. There were many behavioural problems, and children got relentlessly caned. Indeed, the West Indian parents demanded we thrash the boys if they stepped out of line. We will deal with the girls at home, they would say! One of my pupils, Mark, decided the nearby park was too tame for him and managed to set fire to the M32 motorway under construction in the centre of Bristol. He put the project back nine months. He was only ten!

Visiting the homes of some of the difficult kids was a new and rewarding task, and further strengthened my belief that if some kids aren't taken into care, they become dangers to society. They had no support at home.

For most boys of ten or eleven, particularly the West Indian boys who were big for their age, soccer and the school team were their salvation. The school was close to the Bristol Rovers ground, and Bert Tann, the long serving Rovers manager, often came to the school and encouraged the boys, although unlike today, no one from the club came to see the boys play! I ran the school team, which took district championships for several seasons, and enjoyed some good Saturday mornings outside the classroom. Plenty of teacher support but little from the parents!

Everyday teaching at Eastville was stressful and enjoyable, especially when we could see progress in difficult pupils. The stress led to a bout of glandular fever for me in late 1970, and I had to stay at home for one month. During that time, students in their final year were given violins. The result was a lot of squeaky noise, very little tuneful music, and a note from one parent who returned the instrument saying the noise was driving him fucking mad, and please keep the violin in the school. So much for an attempt at bringing culture to the pupils.

Maite and I continued to live in our three-roomed flat in Hanham and drive the speedy but unreliable Hillman Imp. We were saving hard to get a deposit for a house of our own.

Meanwhile, in July 1970, the SS Great Britain returned to Bristol from the Falkland Islands, a ship now visited annually by thousands of tourists. An omen of things to come in the seventies was the dustman strike in Bristol. Angry workers dumped tons of rubbish on the open space known as the Downs. Then in early 1971, decimalisation came to the UK. Also, at the beginning of the new decade, the Campbells paddle steamers, which served the Bristol Channel, South Wales and North Devon Coast, would be withdrawn from service in October 1971. The paddle steamers had existed since Victorian times and were part of West Country history. As they neared the end of their run, Maite and I parked our bikes on the old steamer and travelled to Ilfracombe. From there we did a tour of North Devon and Cornwall till exhaustion, sore bottoms and rain forced us to come back by train to Bristol.

It was good to be back in Bristol after more than five years absence. Old school friends appeared, dinner invites proliferated, and many a fine evening was spent in old friends' company at the Red Lion Inn, at Mangotsfield, on the Gloucestershire side of Bristol. Wives introduced themselves; we were at the 'Four Weddings', not the 'Funeral' side of our lives. Unfortunately, Maite, my wife, was not getting along with my mother, and in turn her mother pushed for us to live in south west France. This move was not possible at this time: the UK had yet to join the European Union. Nevertheless, we pressed on with our jobs with the aim of saving enough money to put a deposit on a house and visit France each summer.

Eastville School became less interesting, and I needed a pay rise so I started looking for promotion to a higher grade of teacher and started selling investment plans while teaching French to adults at evening school. This was a different challenge altogether, and during one of the evening classes I met a remarkable Frenchman who had survived the Algerian War of the fifties and sixties. He was a member of the militia that fought to keep Algeria for the French, and as a commando found himself wounded and captured by the Algerians. After writing a book about his experiences, he was eventually evacuated to France. The French Secret Service raided his home and destroyed the book, threatening him with death if he rewrote it. He panicked and came to live in England, and here he was pretending to learn French at an evening class in Bristol! I enjoyed several good dinners with him.

My efforts to be promoted within the school system eventually paid off, and during the summer term of 1973 I was appointed to a more senior post at Wansdyke Primary School, Whitchurch, Bristol. It was a modern go-ahead school in an aspirant middle-class area. Very few behavioural problems here and a fantastic, self-centred learning culture. I had my own class of nine to eleven-year-olds, and of course ran the school soccer team.

The political and social scene was changing in Britain in the 1970s, and powerful events were to have a significant influence on my future professional and personal life. At Wansdyke I went on strike as a teacher for the first time. The Heath government declared a state of emergency to deal with the docks strike. The Beatles split up at the end of 1970. On January 20, 1971, the first ever postal workers' strike was declared and lasted for forty-seven days. The postal workers lost, and we got no mail. About one year later, on January 9, 1972, the miners' strike started and lasted until February 25. In the same year on July 28, a dockers' strike led to a state of emergency.

It was not all bad. Carrefour, the French hypermarket company, opened their first UK branch in Caerphilly, South Wales. So, at last we could get good French cheese and yogurt. And to help with the finances at the burgeoning supermarkets, on October 23, 1972,

Access credit cards were introduced. Potential opportunities to work in Europe suddenly appeared when on January 1, 1973, the UK entered the EEC or European Community. At least my mother-in-law was pleased.

But with the good, there was the bad. On March 3, 1973, IRA bombs went off in London and by Dec 31, the three-day week was introduced because the lack of coal made it impossible to produce electricity on a twenty-four-hour basis. Inflation for the next three years ranged from 8.4 per cent to 24 per cent. There was much concern in schools and my teachers' union. And it got worse into 1974 as the three-day week continued. During this period, there were two general elections, a state of emergency in Northern Ireland was declared, and the IRA exploded more bombs in mainland Britain. Eventually the three-day week came to an end on March 7,1974 and the OPEC oil embargo finished shortly after on March 19, 1974. There were still the mines negotiations to be settled and agreement was reached in February 1975 when the miners were awarded a thirty-five per cent pay rise by the Conservative government.

There we were, living for most of the above tumultuous times in our little flat with no electricity, heating or water. My thoughts turned to the possibilities of jobs in warmer climates and a new home. But first I had to get my class at Wansdyke into top gear.

During the three years I taught there, I was always amazed at the self-discipline of the pupils, from age five through to eleven. The school ethos looked at the individual and the group. Pupils had their own workbooks for reading, writing and maths, their own story books, and collaborated on many art and craft subjects. If I was late for school or maybe ill, pupils would continue with their work with a minimum of fuss and noise. No one realised I was not there until teatime at ten thirty a.m. Many of the pupils attained very high levels in maths and writing, and often would come back to me from their secondary schools to complain that they were bored and had done all of the work with me, the year before.

I organised the school soccer team, and once again we became local champions but did not manage to win the Bristol Junior Schools Cup. In fact, we did so well that the headmaster, during the daily service, asked the good Lord to wish us well and bless our balls! Needless to say, the staff had to stuff hankies into their mouths to stop their laughter. Not sure if any of the pupils understood the significance of what he said!

One of my class groups during the three years at Wansdyke included three epileptic pupils. Their presence was most unusual and statistically very unlikely. Anyway, Nicholas, the boy who suffered from the worst problems, would suddenly explode without any warning two or three times a week. Fully medicated, he would either attack another pupil, or fall over and hit the ground. I learnt to deal with him, and fortunately he did not set off the other epileptics in the class. They managed to exist on their medication. I often wondered what happened to Nicholas and if he survived into his teenage years.

On one occasion, the school headmaster was absent and his deputy, a lady, took his place in his office. I told her I had split my trousers. Since we were good friends, she told me to come into the office and she would sew them up. I took my trousers off and waited as she looked for her sewing kit. There I was, in the head's office, with the deputy head, no trousers on, and who walks in? The local school inspector. We all blushed and giggled and hope to this day gave him a satisfactory explanation.

After four years of hard saving, Maite and I had enough money to put a deposit on a house in a north Bristol suburb called Patchway. Ironically, it was right next to the runway where they were testing Concorde. The location flashed me back to my days in France and the sonic boom that brought down my bedroom ceiling at the school! It was a pleasant house on a small estate, and we set about furnishing it, and planting the garden. Luckily, we had a few pounds left over, and with Dad's help, bought a minivan. My first new car!

In our first summer, August 1973, we drove to France to see Maite's parents, and left the key to our house with a neighbour. We had a fish tank at the time filled with fish that needed to be fed regularly. Seemed sensible. Unknown to us, our neighbour had a mental problem, and during our absence proceeded to pee in our tank! Why there? The result was a lot of dead fish and some very smelly water. She never came to our house again.

One of my old school friends, Steve, whom I had teacher-trained with, still lived in Bristol and became involved with a religious sect, the Sufis. He took me and Maite to their farm in the Cotswolds for a familiarisation visit. The head man, or guru, of this branch of the sect was called Mike Hurst. For a time, he had sung with a popular UK group called the Springfields. Perhaps their most famous member was Dusty Springfield, who was to die rather tragically in the UK in 1999 aged 59. On the day of our visit, Mike Hurst was not there, and Maite and I were not impressed with the large number of middle-aged ladies who had apparently helped to buy the farm. They took turns receiving sunbeams in the specially constructed garden dome. My friend Steve stuck with them for some time, but Sufism was not for me.

My wife's parents constantly made overtures for their daughter and presumably me to live in France. One day, looking at the Times Education Supplement, out of the blue I saw an advert from Michelin, the tyre company, in Clermont-Ferrand, France. They were looking for international marketing executives, with good English and French, and an educational background. My wife wanted me to apply, so I did and about one month later got an invite to fly to Clermont-Ferrand for an interview.

It was probably the most bizarre interview of my life. The Michelin team never really explained what the job entailed, or where it would be based. At the same time, they recorded all the interviews, and all the candidates sat in an ante room and heard their voices mumbling in the background. I was pleased I did not get the job.

Back in Bristol, Maite discovered she could not have children. We decided to adopt a child, and eventually found little Jonathan in late 1974. He was a light brown in colour and fitted in well with an olive-skinned French woman.

Teaching continued successfully at Wansdyke primary but the UK political and economic situation was alarming. Fond memories of warm weather in France, my in-laws making my wife unhappy and poor relations between my own mother and Maite made me think that it was time to leave the UK for a fresh start. I had hired a colour TV set from Rediffusion in Bristol in early 1975, and by chance saw a series of programmes about Africa, with particular emphasis on Botswana. I was smitten. I loved the colours, the gentle people and dreamed of the warm weather.

Looking through the pages of the Times Educational Supplement, I saw that the UK Overseas Aid Agency was advertising for an in service inspector of schools in guess where? Botswana! This was it. I applied, feeling I was opening a door into new worlds. But at this moment my wife, who supposedly could not get pregnant, told me she was expecting a child. In late 1975, my son Anthony was born with difficulty. My application for a post in Botswana continued into 1976 with interviews in London, medicals, more interviews, and finally acceptance in mid-1976. Just about the time 'Dixon of Dock Green' finished its TV run in Britain, and Harold Wilson left government.

My wife was delighted we were going to leave the UK, despite having two boys under the age of two. My parents were not too keen, especially Dad, who had just retired. My in-laws fumed that we would now be even further away! My friends gathered around us and helped us get ready, while by chance the Overseas Aid Agency introduced me to a Tswana citizen who was studying at Bristol University. Gladstone Pilane and I became firm friends. He was the vice principal of the teachers' college in Francistown, Botswana. Gladstone gave me many tips about living in his country, and handed me a good letter of introduction to his family in both Botswana and South Africa. Gladstone was from a royal tribal family.

My last term at Wansdyke Primary School quickly came to an end. The house was let out to officers from the Argentinian Air Force, who were test flying aircraft from the nearby aerodrome. Eventually of course they would have to leave when Britain declared war on Argentina. More on that later.

Suitcases and trunks were packed and unpacked, and the little boys became very excited. After a pleasant

Christmas lunch with my parents, we set off for Heathrow Airport on December 27, 1979. It was a very cold day. My friend Sandy had lent us her Morris Minor, and a few other friends followed behind with the rest of our luggage.

We flew British Airways in a Boeing 747 to Johannesburg. The plane was only six years old and we had four seats with two cots for the boys. Unfortunately, we missed a trip by boat from Southampton to Cape Town, a service that had just been withdrawn. Never mind — the long flight was our first. We slept most of the way.

The plane doors opened in Johannesburg, and we were struck by the blinding light of an African summer. The heat in the airport building was overwhelming. Air conditioning not very good in 1976 in Johannesburg. We got to the front of the immigration queue where I noticed the officer gazing at my adopted son Jonathan, who was of mixed race. He examined the passport several times and finally let us all through the barrier to the luggage carousel.

This was South Africa only six months after the Soweto riots of 1976. Tension was still high. We had been booked into the Airport Holiday Inn, a so-called multiracial hotel, for guests from outside South Africa. We were to stay for two nights before flying on to Gaborone, the capital of Botswana. The first morning I woke up at dawn, just before six a.m. in Johannesburg in mid-summer, and the light coming through the curtains was warm and blinding. I could hear the sound of footsteps outside the hotel as workers walked by. Just like Lancashire and the clogs of the 1950s.

The breakfast table was astonishing for a family which had not stayed in many upmarket hotels. Any meat dish was possible, including minced steak! I had never seen people eat steak for breakfast, but the locals, all white, preferred it to bacon with their eggs. We spent the day at the hotel, and the boys loved paddling in the pool. Just forty-eight hours out of the freezing UK!

Everybody was dead tired. South African time was two hours ahead of the UK, and we were at an altitude of nearly fifteen hundred metres. The flight to Gaborone in Botswana was early on December 30, 1976, and we had a lot of luggage. The plane flew a little late, but we arrived in Gaborone, the capital of Botswana, just before midday. It was hotter than Jo'burg, two hundred and fifty kilometres to the south, and on the edge of the Kalahari Desert. We were met at the airport by the project leader, Mr Bram Swallow, a former headteacher from the UK. He drove us in his Land Rover to the Gaborone Holiday Inn, where we were to spend the next five days, including New Year's Eve and New Year's Day. Luckily, the hotel was air conditioned; the oppressive heat kept the children awake.

At first the boys were reluctant to run on the hotel lawns because they were frightened of snakes that they said were also in the pools. Anyway, the fear passed, and they began to have a good time, quickly making friends. Most of the guests were black and very curious about meeting a French woman, her white and black children, and her English husband.

Botswana by 1976 had been independent for ten years and its national flag displayed bands of blue water, black for its black citizens and white for its white folk. Botswana, a democracy formerly called Bechuanaland, had for nearly a century been the home for white folk escaping from South Africa and for Europeans, particularly Jews who had fled Europe in the early 1900s. Relationships between all races were good and in 1976, the speaker of the house of parliament was Mr Jimmy Haskins, whose family had gone to Bechuanaland in the late 1890s from Warmley, Bristol. I got to know Jimmy, who lived in Francistown, and amazingly, on his visits back to Bristol he had met several of my school friends.

There we were, stuck in an African hotel for New Year 1976. A good time to try and get used to the country and prepare ourselves for our trip north by train to Francistown, where we would be based. Eventually on Jan 3, 1977, it seemed like years had passed since we left England when a Land Rover came to the hotel to take us to Gaborone Station. Today, forty years on, this station, which was merely a halt with a ticket office, is now in the centre of town and surrounded by office blocks and several hotels.

A porter loaded our cases and trunks into the luggage van on the Rhodesian railway train that had come from Mahikeng and was bound for Francistown and Bulawayo, in Rhodesia. At that time Botswana had no locomotives or drivers of its own. The journey was a slow one of about four hundred and two kilometres across the edge of the Kalahari, through the night, and into Francistown early in the morning. At every stop, the soundtrack changed as people sold food, artefacts and goats, and tried to force themselves onto the train.

There were first, second and third class carriages. At that time, the conductor was usually of Scottish ancestry and his team of black chefs produced miraculous foods for the evening meal and breakfast. The latter was always bacon and eggs and the most delicious porridge. Upon arrival in Francistown, an officious-looking station official, not the first I was going to meet in Botswana, saw my luggage and confiscated it, claiming its entry into Botswana had not been declared. We walked on foot to our hotel, the Francistown, now demolished, which was to be our home for the next three weeks or so, while the local authority searched for a house for us. We told our story to the clerk who was expecting the Welch family, and she was able to retrieve some of our luggage from the recalcitrant railway official.

Francistown is now a city of over a hundred thousand people and the second largest town in Botswana. Today there are many fine hotels, but in 1976, there was the Francistown and the Tati. The latter was indeed tatty, so we ended up in the better option, the Francistown, at the top of the main street. The room was certainly bigger than the one in the Gaborone Holiday Inn, but the air conditioning was as erratic as the electricity.

I phoned my boss, Mr Bram Swallow in Gaborone, to say we had arrived and were awaiting a house. It won't take long he said, and I will send you my colleague, Mr Sola, to come and help you with any local problems. After a week or so, the boys were restless in a hotel without a pool, and all we could do all day was to walk around what was then a small town with two hotels, two banks, one post office, lots of bazaars, and one garage. Eventually, a phone call gave us great joy: the housing department had found a house for us. And as if by magic, my new colleague, Mr Sola, re-emerged with a Land Rover and drove us to a large colonial house on the edge of town. It was three times the size of our house in Bristol, with a big garden and servants' quarters. We had never had them before, nor imagined the problems that servants and gardeners were to bring.

The house was full of cockroaches in the bottle gas-powered kitchen and had a hot water system called a Rhodesian boiler. This system was fired by wood in its boiler to produce the daily supply of hot water for showers and washing. We managed to unpack all of our cases and trunks, and next day got a lift into town to purchase necessary items like a fridge and crockery. A few days later, a friendly colleague from the Agricultural Department nearby lent me his battered old

Land Rover, so we could get around town and I could visit my new offices in the education department compound.

At the end of January 1977, Botswana was enduring a heat wave and exceptionally heavy rains that always seemed to descend at three o'clock in the afternoon. In fact, it rained so heavily that year, and again in 1978, that the roads were continually flooded for more than two years. Needless to say, neither my house nor the office was fully waterproofed or air conditioned. It took some time to acclimatise to damp summer heat. A colleague, who had been sent further north to Maun, told me he took three months to adjust from the English winter he had just left. I had been promised a Land Rover so that I could visit the schools in Botswana and do in service training work with the teachers. Its arrival from UK via Cape Town and Gaborone was somewhat delayed, so I bought a Renault 4, assembled in Rhodesia, from a German vet called Klaus. He had decided to leave Rhodesia and its troubles and settle in Botswana. It was a fantastic little car with a gear stick in the dashboard and high ground clearance. It would go almost everywhere a Land Rover would go.

I had gone from being a primary school teacher to an inspector of schools in Botswana. It became clear to me that expatriates led their lives on the grand scale in the former colonies. Overseas allowances seemed to go further, there were always parties on the weekend, and life revolved around the Francistown Club, one of the oldest in Botswana, with a magnificent clubhouse and bar, golf course, cricket pitch and many other facilities. Many of the locals would leave their offices at five p.m. and head straight to the club to start downing the local brew. For the South African expatriates, and there were many who ran the businesses in Francistown, life was easy with plenty of workmen and help at home. The children and my wife settled in well, and she started a play school from our home. Bringing up children in Africa is a dream. There is almost always sunshine and they can be outdoors most of the time.

New to African life, finding maids and gardeners was not so easy in Botswana, and we fell into every trap. Neighbours would suggest a maid or gardener, but without references making the right choice was always difficult. Our first maid, Judea, unknown to us, was pregnant, so slowly her work rate diminished. She cooked tripe which smelled terribly and after giving birth demanded we pay her pregnancy leave. The first part time gardener turned out to be a thief who stole my portable radio. The scenario continued until we found reasonable people who turned out to be Rhodesians, born with great practical and gardening skills.

Francistown is close to the Rhodesian border and was continuously targeted by the so-called white Rhodesian forces as a haven for terrorists or terrs, as they called them locally. There was a refugee camp nearby for Rhodesians who had escaped across the border, mainly people from the leading tribe called Shona. From this camp, the men were trained as soldiers and then returned via Zambia, so most of the refugees were women and children. Schools in the camp taught the Zimbabwean curriculum, much to the annoyance of the Botswana authorities.

Francistown was full of United Nations, US Aid, Danish Aid and various church aid societies, in fact, any organisation that helped refugees or displaced persons. The so-called white Rhodesian army, actually more than seventy-five percent black, were aware of the recruitment and care of future soldiers in Francistown, and often dropped leaflets urging all Rhodesians to go home. They occasionally mounted lightning attacks across the Botswana border, targeting political or military leaders who were hiding out in the locality. One of the high-level Rhodesians, Mr Dumisa Dabengwa, lived opposite me and we chatted occasionally over the fence. His nickname was the Black Russian. No need to say where he got his military training. When he eventually left Francistown in 1979, workers cleared his house and dug up the garden to find bodies and arms under the sandy soil.

My office was located alongside the main dirt road from Francistown to Bulawayo in Rhodesia. Sitting at my desk one day, I heard voices coming towards me. I looked up and saw several hundred black school kids running from the Bulawayo direction. These were children who had run away from Rhodesia and were seeking sanctuary in Botswana. Before the kids had passed me, my phone rang. It was a British journalist, based in Johannesburg, who heard about the exodus and wanted a story. I told him to get up to Francistown himself as my status as a British government officer meant I could not comment. Needless to say, he ran a story which told about kids being wounded, shot in the back, etc. Nonsense, not one of them had been harmed. I was there.

I worked as an education officer, giving workshops and courses to update the skills of the Tswana primary teachers. I visited local schools near the Rhodesian border on many occasions and witnessed many events and occasionally was shot at. All these events were reported to the British High Commission in Gaborone, but it never reacted.

Despite the war in Rhodesia, I visited that beautiful country, and my wife and I decided to head for Victoria Falls. We all set out in our Renault 4L, across the sandy bush dirt road for Bulawayo, the nearest big Rhodesian town. As we neared it, we could not believe what we were seeing. Here was a modern town with all modern conveniences. There was a Holiday Inn, and in Dowling's Bakery we found the best cream cakes we had ever tasted. Everything was so cheap. At that time, the Rhodesian Tourist Authority was running massively subsidized trips to the Falls. These Flame Lily trips cost about five Rhodesian dollars for four people!

The road from Bulawayo to Vic Falls went through the bush where there was plenty of wildlife, and reputedly plenty of terrorists as well! The distance was about four hundred and fifty kilometres and the Flame Lily tour representative said we would travel by bus in an armed convoy and leave our car in Bulawayo. The journey lasted about six hours, and we saw neither terrorists nor elephants! We stayed in a rest camp near the Falls and enjoyed a barbecue or braai as the locals called it. When we arrived at night, we could hear the water but not see it. After breakfast in the morning, we walked to the falls and were dumbstruck by its width and the volume of water cascading over it. We spent the day looking at the falls from various vantage points and playing with the boys at some distance from the edge. We did not cross into the Zambian side but got a look at the famous Elephant Hills Golf Course.

Next day, it was time to go, and we boarded our small bus which had double axles at the back. I thought this was strange at the time but it was to prove useful, if not lifesaving. The driver had elected to drive to Bulawayo without a convoy after hearing the route was safe at that time.

After about fifty kilometres there was a huge bang, and the bus skidded across the road. I thought we had been hit by a rocket. Finally, we stopped and although I expected more explosions, there were none. The driver told us to stay in the bus, grabbed his pistol, walked around the bus and discovered a burst tyre on one of the double axles. No rocket propelled grenade! But we were now alone in the middle of the bush. No convoy this time, and it was obvious he could not repair the tyre alone. But suddenly help arrived in the shape of a Rhodesian farmer in a Ford Cortina who was driving to Vic Falls. He pulled up, looked around, took his rifle and walked towards the bus. Eventually he and the driver decided they could remove the damaged tyre and replace it with a new one. However, they wanted cover in case the terrorists attacked, so I was deputed to lie down in the road with the rifle and shoot at anybody who approached and who looked suspicious. Luckily, no one appeared, and after about thirty minutes we were able to continue our ride back to Bulawayo.

Other trips to Rhodesia became more hazardous as the end of the end of the war was close and there was much military activity. On one train trip from Bulawayo to Salisbury, or Harare, as it is now known, it was obvious the locomotive had been shot at, and the train was loaded with soldiers. Some passengers were worried about land mines on the track. I had a friend, the rugby coach to the Francistown rugby team, who lived just over the border in Rhodesia. He owned a trading store and illegally changed Botswana pula to Rhodesian dollars for me when I needed spares for the Rhodesian built Renault 4L. Rhodesia's educational standard for white and black was high, and I was privileged to meet informed, intriguing people living in the bush on massive farms or trading posts.

Back in Francistown, my Land Rover Defender had arrived, and I began to visit schools to talk to teachers and show them various teaching aids. I was soon joined by my Danish friend, Bengt Jorgensen, who ran a teaching and production unit in Francistown. Full of life, Bengt enjoyed a drink, a sandwich, and a conversation. Our fame began to spread, and we soon had requests to visit schools all over the northern part of Botswana. Remember, Botswana is the same size as France, about seventy per cent desert and has a population of just over two million.

A daunting task faced Bengt and me. We had once visited Maun in the Okavango Delta, for a teachers' workshop, got very drunk and showered in black tap water. We then drove my Land Rover through people's gardens and snapped plenty of washing lines. Bras and underpants festooned the car.

Eventually, we saw a strange-looking house and stopped. Inside, we met an odd-looking couple who welcomed us into their home and offered us drink and girls! No, we did not stay. Aids had still not reached Botswana, but we made a run for it and drove off back through the gardens to Riley's Inn, the only hotel in town. Maun in the late 1970s was still Botswana's wild west where locals rode horses into town and tethered them outside Riley's Inn.

My wife was becoming disgruntled with my trips away from home to the desert and bush. Also, I was often called to head office in Gaborone which meant a journey of two nights on the train and several days in a hotel in the capital. She was alone with the boys for long periods, but from now on, my professional life would be both in education and unknown to me, television. More of that later.

The train journeys in Botswana were always slow and interesting. The carriages had all been custom made in the UK for Rhodesian railways, and the locomotives were diesel powered. At that time, Botswana had no railway equipment or staff of its own, relying on Rhodesian railways for all of its works, including drivers, conductors, station masters, engineers, etc. As they were all white and Rhodesia was at war with black terrorists, the situation often led to short term arrests of the railway folk who were accused of being spies. The local Botswana police got very confused about the number of strangers in town, and I was arrested at my home one night during a party! The inspector at my door accused me of being a British spy but was soon confronted by my local guests and told to go away. All he really wanted was a drink or two and some food. We obliged!

The train journeys from Francistown to the capital, Gaborone, and back were mostly at night and usually started with a beer in the bar followed by dinner in the restaurant car, cooked by the black chefs, and then back to the carriage for a few hours' sleep as the train clicked its way through the night, stopping at many halts and small towns. You never knew who would share your carriage. I met many of the top civil servants in Botswana, including the deputy vice president, who incidentally was Sir Seretse Khama's brother. At that time, Seretse had been president since independence in 1966 and had frightened the surrounding South Africans by marrying a white woman.

The crowning glory of the rail trip was breakfast at about six a.m. with the immense bright light flooding into the restaurant car. From a tiny space, the chefs produced porridge, bacon, eggs, sausage and toast, along with Rhodesian coffee or tea. Magnificent! The days in Gaborone were always busy at the Ministry of Education, discussing projects and addressing teachers' meetings. Interesting times working with people who wanted to improve their teaching levels.

Usually we headed back to Francistown on the Friday night train, arriving home at about eight a.m. The train, as at all stations, was surrounded by locals selling all types of food and trinkets. For us, it was time to see the family and prepare for a barbecue or braai weekend. On one of these barbecue weekends, I almost got bitten by a snake. The puff adder had buried itself in the dirt near the house, but luckily I saw its shape before I put my foot on it. Highly poisonous snakes are very common in Botswana and without an immediate antidote can be fatal. Just one of the hazards of living in that kind of country.

There were four of us providing in service teacher training throughout Botswana with our leader based in

Gaborone. We were a team requested by the Botswana government and operated about six thousand miles away from London, where our paymasters were based. One day, we got a message to meet a UK government representative in Francistown, along with all the other officers seconded from the UK and based in northern Botswana. We did not know why he was coming or what he wanted to say to us. As the meeting began it became obvious his news from London wasn't good. The UK economy was struggling, and he had to announce a proposed reduction in our salary of ten per cent. The room went quiet for about five seconds and then erupted as though everybody had been stung by a puff adder. Who do you think you are! No fucking way! Get back to London. The bureaucrat was escorted out of the Francistown Hotel, and we never saw him again. Don't think our salaries were reduced! Incredible that a government would try that trick.

An interesting primary school had developed in the desert town of Orapa, north west of Francistown. The town had been built to mine diamonds by De Beers, and this it did twenty-four hours a day. Everything was brought in by road. Houses were built, reservoirs were dug out of the desert, a small airport constructed. Schools, hotels and guest houses, and roads were all miraculously established in this remote part of the Kalahari Desert. I was invited to give an In Service course to the teachers working at the mine, and it was very pleasant in the company of interested teachers, with a pleasant social life after work. After the headmaster decided to move to Cape Town, I was asked to apply for his job by the mine manager. I did not get it and no doubt the gods were looking my way. I might have spent a further twenty years in the desert! Orapa was a great place to visit, but the road to the mine was full of potholes and large numbers of trucks carrying provisions. Not for the faint-hearted or those without a Land Rover!

Further north of Francistown was the Okavango Delta, the town of Maun, the Caprivi Strip which has borders with Botswana, Angola and Namibia, and of course the rest of the Kalahari Desert. Many schools in these remote areas had never been visited or inspected since independence in 1966. My colleague Ted and I loaded our Land Rovers with all of our teaching equipment, food, two hundred litres of water and about three hundred litres of fuel and set off from Maun towards the small town of Toteng on the edge of the Okavango Delta and not far from Lake Ngami. This lake was famously visited by David Livingstone in 1849, who described it as shimmering, some eighty miles long and twenty miles wide. On that day, late in 1978, the lake was only about one metre deep in most places, and we were able to drive our Land Rovers across it. The Okavango main delta to the north of Lake Ngami feeds some of its precious water into the lake. The Okavango inland delta itself is described as one of the wonders of the world and is certainly one of the world's biggest inland deltas. Many varieties of wildlife and plants flourish during the wet season, and there are huge patches of green everywhere.

Ted and I were heading for Sehitwa on the far side of Lake Ngami to inspect several primary schools, which had not been visited for decades. Since it was difficult to contact these schools in advance — no mobile phones or many landlines in those days — our arrival was unexpected. We camped the night in the school office where there was just enough space to install our portable stretcher beds. The headmaster killed a cow, and as a special treat offered us the liver. Not for me I'm afraid, but I did manage to eat a small piece to keep everybody happy. The lady teachers cooked local vegetables, and in the morning, made delicious millet porridge for the two of us. We put on a good day course for the teachers, and next day set off to the south west away from the Okavango towards the Kalahari and a small town called Ghanzi. This town of about twelve thousand people was a trading centre, cattle raising area, and Bushman town. Above all, it was a very ethnically mixed town, with South African Boers having emigrated there in 1897/98. They brought their cattle; the climate, despite being semi-arid, could support grazing for large herds.

Ted and I, after a long dusty drive across the Kalahari, pulled up at the aptly named Kalahari Arms Hotel. First thing we needed was a couple of beers each! We booked rooms for two nights, found out where the local primary school was located, met some of the locals in the bar, and continued with our beers. Suddenly, at about seven p.m., the owner of the hotel announced that he had run out of beer, but never mind, he would dash down to the airstrip, crank up his plane and pick up more brew in Namibia. Unsure of what to believe, Ted and I decided to follow him to the airstrip, where in an instant, he took off. We waited for about forty-five minutes and then out of the night sky saw a small plane approaching, dipping its wings in triumph. We offloaded our beers into one of our government Land Rovers, strictly illegal of course, and returned to the Kalahari Arms. A great roar of approval went up as we carried beer into the bar. This is still the only time in my life that I have had my beer delivered by aeroplane!

Ted and I later strolled into the hotel restaurant and of course ordered steak and chips, all that was available! Ted, being a traditional Englishman, decided to ask for horseradish sauce. I was embarrassed and told him not to bother. However, to my amazement, and here we were in the middle of the Kalahari, six thousand miles from the UK, the one and only waiter did not protest but simply returned with a pot of the sauce. Maybe a few other Brits had passed that way before.

Next day, after a good egg and boerewors sausage breakfast, Ted and I went to the local primary school. The teachers were very keen to talk about their teaching problems such as lack of books, teaching aids, and actual classrooms. Some teachers were actually working outside under a friendly tree or bush. Still the kids seemed happy, and it was interesting to see Bushman children integrating with the other local kids.

Time to move on, so after a petrol fill-up at the local government depot and provisions from the trading store, we set off on the long drive of about six hundred km to Lobatse on the southern side of Botswana. We would pass though Kang, Sekoma and Kanye. There was no proper road, just a dirt track, and I had no maps. But it was not easy to get lost. It actually rained during our two-day trip and at once green shoots and small flowers appeared everywhere. A strange sensation.

My Land Rover was bouncing up and down on the dirt track when suddenly there was a bang, and one of the front shock absorber elements came loose. As I slowed down and got out, I realised that I did not have the tools to be able to jack the car up and tighten the offending part. Darkness was coming, so Ted and I realised the only thing we could do was to make camp and wait for someone to come along. This protocol was the safety advice given to those who broke down in remote places.

After about thirty minutes, we heard an engine noise, and out of a cloud of dust came a massive cattle truck obviously on its way to the meat processing plant in Lobatse. When the driver caught sight of us, he slowed down and eventually stopped. He asked what was wrong, saw we were in government vehicles and in his bad English/Afrikaans accent, offered to help. We explained what was wrong once again, and he decided to make camp with us, let all the animals off his truck so they could graze, and yanked all of his heavy-duty tools off the truck. He was able to jack up the car, fix the loose part, and then share our dinner in the bush. We had a fun evening, swapping stories, with him telling us about his life in the bush. He was proud of his swimming pool and small plane of his own. A different life from a teacher in Bristol.

In the morning, the cattle driver got all of his beef herd onto his truck and left before us. He stirred up a tremendous dust plume with fifty tonnes of beef on board. Later next day, we pulled into Lobatse in southern Botswana, shaken and dusty from the dirt road and desperate for a bath. At that time Botswana had few tar roads, so the arrival in Lobatse always felt good, with about a hundred kilometres of good road in front of us. But first a bath at the Cumberland Hotel and a meeting with our local colleague, Gerald. To get to the hotel, we drove past the Botswana Commission Meat Factory plant, aware of the odour that pervaded Lobatse: cooked meat.

Other trips in Botswana took me to the Limpopo region in the south east corner of the country. This area backed onto South Africa, and there were several river crossings between the two countries. On a particular trip, besides visiting schools, I was also delivering garden equipment which central government had failed to deliver.

At the school, I met the headmaster and was told he had been arrested for stealing oranges growing by the river. I spoke to the magistrate and got the headmaster released on condition he gave back the bags of oranges and would return to school with me. Needless to say, the poor fellow agreed, and we set off for the school, where I spent the night. In the morning, I delivered the forks and spades, had a porridge breakfast with the wayward headmaster, and he promptly gave me two bags of oranges as a present. No doubt these were stolen so I decided to get out of there very quickly in my government vehicle.

On the way back to Francistown, I decided to pay a visit to some schools in the town of Selebi-Phikwe. This was a modern coal mining town with a large stretch of tar road linking to the main dirt road to Francistown and Gaborone. Not far from Phikwe, as dusk approached, I spotted cows on the road, a common occurrence in Botswana. Too late I realised that I was going to hit one of the animals, still lying in the middle of the road. I heard a God-almighty bang; the cow hit the front bumper and came up over the bonnet, just stopping before the windscreen. Luckily for me. It could have decapitated me and my passenger. Slowly, as the Land Rover reduced speed, the cow fell off the bonnet and onto the side of the road. I motored on for a mile or so, but became aware of a tinkling noise coming from the engine. The car also smelt as if it was running hot!

Besides pushing the cast iron fender into the car, the cow had damaged the radiator and the water pump. I stopped the car, which was slowly losing power, and turned around to where I had left the cow, but it had disappeared. Just a few traces of blood! I looked into the dusky gloom as night was now falling and saw a group of locals busy cutting up the carcass! Good meat never goes to waste in Botswana, even if you don't own it! I managed to get the Land Rover started again and finally arrived at my friend Bob's house where I was due to spend the night. He thought the accident with the cow was a real laugh and decided that the Land Rover would have to be repaired by the government transport office before I could return to Francistown. The work meant a few days stay in Phikwe with a possible rugby game and after that, no doubt, a party and braai.

The rugby game came and went, and in fact was the last competitive game I played. My back could not take it any more. After the game, drinking began, and the food included a strange-looking cake! Later I found out that the cake was laced with ganja or dagga. It wasn't only the locals who consumed the local weed, but the expats as well. I had never before smoked or eaten dagga, and never since. I found the experience strange, and it made me dizzy. Quite a few of the guests, no doubt, were smoking the stuff and eating the cake. Strange things were happening. The front of one lady's white tee shirt was covered with fingerprints. Pursued by a lot of guys, she seemed oblivious to what was happening.

My good friend Bob, a maths teacher from Bristol, let me stay with him for a few days whilst my Land Rover was repaired. Later, in mid-1978, Bob and I made a trip to Johannesburg. This was two years after the Soweto riots, and South Africa now seemed a strained and strange place to me. We went to a pop concert in Benoni, a suburb to the east of Johannesburg, and did not see one black person. One night, our hosts in Benoni heard a knock on the door and found an armed policeman on the doorstep. He said there were thieves around and reminded us it was all right to shoot them. The cops would come and clean up later. We wouldn't be charged! Astonishing! Bob and I drove back to Botswana thanking our lucky stars we lived in a peaceful country. A few petty thieves, but not much violent crime.

I eventually picked up my Land Rover from the government garage in Botswana and went home to Francistown. My wife was not very happy with all my absences and travel, and said she wanted to go back to Europe. We split up and lived separately for a time. During this period, I was approached by publishers MacMillan Boleswa to write a series of social study readers for primary schools in Botswana. The books were to be called Zebra Readers, and there would be fifteen in total. Since I did not see my children every day, I had plenty of time. I shared a flat with the local librarian called Andrew, a South African political exile. I completed the books in three months and eventually they sold about five hundred thousand copies over a period of about five years, an enormous number. The readers seemed to be in every school I visited.

My time in Botswana was slowly coming to an end. I liked the country, wanted to stay, and had a new girlfriend who happened to be black. Many of the expatriates did not like this relationship, and the poison of this racism even infected my employers at Overseas Aid. They reported my situation to my local employers, the Botswana government. Authorities called me to Gaborone after concluding that I had three months to serve on my contract, and should complete it. At the same time, my passport expired and the British Consul in Gaborone refused to renew it unless I agreed to leave Botswana. Here my father, furious about how I was being treated, intervened on my behalf. My father was friendly with a Bristol MP called Michael Cocks, who was chief whip of the Labour Party. Michael used diplomatic channels to ask why my passport was being withheld, and it did not take long for it to appear without any threats of my instant removal from Botswana. To this day, despite my world travels ever since, I have little respect for the treatment of British citizens overseas by their own officials.

My wife had decided to spend a few more months in Botswana, so I booked my return trip to UK via Athens, Greece. I had always wanted to visit Greece, and as part of my trip took a ferry to some of the Greek isles. Little did I know I would return fourteen years later to set up Greek pay TV. But more on that later.

It was 1980 and Greece was soon to enter the European Union. People felt much optimism. I stayed near the Acropolis, managing to avoid the prostitutes in the local bars, but meet up with a Syrian lady and her daughter. They were very cultured, French-speaking, wealthy and on their way to Paris for shopping. We had some nice meals together. Then it was time to say goodbye to them, and I headed for London. My father picked me up and said he was glad to see me home. He did not like Botswana, but might be tempted to visit South Africa, which he had passed through and liked. My mother waited anxiously in Bristol for news of her grandchildren, but not of her soon to be former daughter-in-law. It was now October, and I had still had to sort out my final pay and bonus in London with my employers. What a pleasure dealing with them. After three years in Botswana, I couldn't believe UK civil servants answered the phone and responded to written requests. Next up was my house in Bristol, which my father had managed to sell but there was still paperwork to be done.

I had come back to Europe without a renewed contract in Africa, but had no intention of working in England again. I had fallen in love with Africa. I started looking in all the educational journals for posts. I applied for some with private institutions, suspecting the UK government would not employ me again after my marital problems in Botswana. Meanwhile, Christmas was coming, and I was too old to work for the post office as I had during my late teens. I saw an advert in the Bristol Evening Post for temporary work at Victoria Wine Stores, and luckily, I managed to get a job in their Bedminster branch, not far from the old Wills Tobacco Factory district in Bristol. By then, Wills had moved their main factory and headquarters to the Hartcliffe area.

The manager of the branch, a man in his early sixties, cleverly looked at all the applicants and chose a doctor, vet, teacher and engineer as his temporary staff. We were all between jobs or just graduating, and could handle all the work with ease. The manager, I'll call him Jim, soon realised these varied skills were to his advantage and often gave us the shop keys and access to the till. He would come to work later on in the morning and take over the late shopping hours. Jim often wished we could all stay at the shop on a permanent basis. But January 2, 1980 put a stop to that as sales plummeted and we were no longer needed. The store had been close to the catchment area of my last British school, and it was strange to meet as customers former parents and teachers from the school. Everybody in the nearly four years I had been away was either divorced or getting divorced. Some of the parents were only a few years older than me, and it was fun to see them as customers, and not mums and dads.

I spent Christmas with my parents in Bristol and visited my aunts and uncles, who were all still alive and living in the area. For new year I visited my long time French friend, Patrice, in Lille. He always celebrated with his university friends: champagne and oysters were the order of the day, and the good times brought back memories of my first visit to France in 1960, and my quest to find a properly cooked steak!

Returning to England in early January 1980, I found a letter from the University of the Witwatersrand in Johannesburg. I had written to them in response to an advert requesting a research monitor for an English language teaching project in Soweto. Unknown to me, this was a UK British Council project. Wits, as the university was called, liked the work I had done and wanted to interview me at their London office. I met a charming lady who decided to offer me a three-month consultancy on the spot. At this time, four years after the Soweto riots, the Johannesburg black townships of Soweto and Alexandra were not very safe places, but I was assured I could get a permit to visit the schools in the project and return safely to my office in central Johannesburg. Wits also assured me they could get me a South African entry visa for a limited stay. About a week later I was on the plane back to Johannesburg.

The Wits campus was and still is vast and close to the centre of Johannesburg. We had our offices in a remote part of the campus, away from the main centres of learning. Looking back, I think the university authorities wanted to keep this suspicious project, sponsored by the British Council, away from prying eyes. The local team that met me consisted entirely of ladies. At that time, they would have been classed as liberals who had more contact with black people than the average white person who only knew his maid and gardener. Indeed, one of the ladies had a child with a black colleague and went to great lengths to keep the forbidden relationship hidden. This lady belonged to a group of friends who had all crossed the colour line and met secretly at each other's homes. Apartheid was at its height in the early 1980s, and security police were everywhere. Still to come was the bombing of the ANC headquarters in London in 1982, and the death of activist Neil Aggett in Johannesburg in 1982 as well. Unknown to me, the security police were looking into my background in Botswana and my relationship with a black woman.

The so-called white suburbs were still very quiet and well policed, so their inhabitants were often unaware of turmoil in the black townships. I took over the end of an unexpired lease on a flat in Caroline Street, Hillbrow, a lively upmarket suburb close to the university campus. I was able to walk to work in complete safety and saw the ladies from the Black Sash, silently demonstrating against apartheid at major intersections, often getting abused by drivers who waited at the lights. One evening, very late, I walked home and was accosted by a black boy who simply said he wanted to talk to me, and I should not beat him. As we walked along Claim Street past all the restaurants, he asked me for money for food. Unlike today, Hillbrow was calm then, but today is a centre of high crime, unemployment, poverty and people from all over Africa.

As my research and monitoring of the Soweto English language project continued, I made several accompanied visits to schools in Soweto and the other black township called Alexandra. I always had my official permit to visit these areas; at any time the police could stop me and ask what I was doing. Without a permit I could be removed at once. The townships during my visits seemed tense, but I did not see any major incidents or feel any aggression towards myself. The teachers in the schools were very helpful, as were the pupils.

After about two months, Professor Don White, who was overseeing the project, called me in for a chat and told me that my work was good, but authorities would not extend my work visa. No reasons were given, but I had guessed why: Botswana had caught up with me. Anyway, Don White said he had someone I should meet who perhaps could help me stay in Africa. He gave me Dr Jacques Kriel's phone number and said I should speak to this man.

I had reached a turning point in my life. Jacques Kriel, Afrikaner he might be, had realised that South Africa would be destroyed if people of all races and colours did not work and live together. Dr Kriel at this time was the minister of health, in one of the black homelands, called Bophuthatswana — let's call it Bop from now on. Bop was centred around Mahikeng, famed for the Boer War and Baden-Powell and was principally in the north west of South Africa. Dr Kriel had a vision. He wanted to start a university for all races in Mahikeng, and he had the support of the president of the homeland, Mr Lucas Mangope. Besides that, the South African government had plenty of money at this time; the rand was worth more than the dollar.

I drove up to Mahikeng, about two hundred and fifty kilometres from Johannesburg, met Jacques Kriel and accepted a post of lecturer at the new university. Lecturer in what? Nobody knew at this time. My main job was to plan the university, which had the land and money to move forward. Two other guys were appointed, one as a senior lecturer in economics and the other as the university registrar. We found an office in town above a tyre garage, called Calgen House. For the next two years, this location would be the central university office. Some houses were being built on the university site, but none were finished, so I moved into the Crewes Hotel by the station in Mahikeng. The hotel was run by three widows Crewes, whose age varied from forty to eighty-six. Granny Crewes, who was alive during the Boer War, told me of her war experiences and how she had a photo taken of herself sitting with Baden-Powell. The other two Crewes widows had both lost their husbands in road accidents. I spent about three months in this hotel and was eventually joined by the new professor of English, Derrick Nuttall. He had just retired as the head of the British Council and later introduced me to the Freemasons in Mahikeng. Together, the small team, with Dr Kriel at the head, commissioned research and architects to plan the very best for the university. Teaching aids were just coming into use, and one of my first tasks was to ensure that the new lecture theatres could use all the latest audio-visual materials.

Mahikeng, as it is now called, had periods of drought, which could last three or four years, alternating with periods of high rainfall. During 1980 and 1981, the rains poured down, and the building site became a mud bath on a more or less permanent basis. We put up temporary Portakabin offices and lecture rooms as the main buildings were still under construction. The first students also arrived early in 1981, many of them from Soweto. These students were astonished to find a growing multiracial staff from all over the world, and even more so, white staff with whom they could talk. Many students told me that this was the first time they had managed a proper conversation with a white person. Astonishing! The level of English and the paucity of study skills of these students was daunting, so we started remedial courses in English and activated the use of the library and reference books. Remember this period was some time before computers became available.

I had moved from the hotel and shared a house on the campus with Johan de Villiers Graaf and his wife, both lecturers at the university. Johan was the son of De Villiers Graaf, the then liberal leader of the political opposition in South Africa. Sir De Villiers Graaf had a hereditary knighthood, a legacy from his grandfather, who had assisted the British during the Boer War. There we were, all back in Mahikeng, the most famous Boer War town! The university also appointed numerous other persons, whose liberal views aroused suspicion in South Africa. Bop or Bophuthatswana had abolished apartheid and allowed freedom of speech. In President Lucas Mangope, they had a very enlightened leader, even though he was castigated by the African National Congress for taking the white man's shilling or rand.

Meanwhile, at the end of 1980, my girlfriend Patricia, later to be my second wife, gave birth to my daughter in Gaborone. I went to pick up Patricia and Tumelo in Botswana, and on the way back we stopped to help a motorist who happened to be Ian Khama, the son of the then President of Botswana, Sir Seretse Khama. Little did we know that Khama would himself become president of Botswana, many years later.

At the border with three gates — Botswana, South Africa and Bophuthatswana — we sailed through the first two with our newborn child, but were refused admittance into Bophuthatswana. Luckily, the permanent secretary for home affairs was one of my students, and so we phoned him from the border post, and he arrived with his inkpad and rubber stamp. We passed through and went to our newly finished house. What a relief!

Slowly, the university buildings took shape and more staff and students arrived. The rector of the university, now Professor John Makhene, one of the most able men I have ever met, realised that besides the learning problems of the students, the lecturers needed help with their teaching methods. Many of them were just plain boring! I was asked to set up the Instructional Development Centre, or IDC, to provide staff with teaching aids and instructional planning. I appointed a secretary, a graphic artist, and an engineer/technician to repair all the gear we purchased for the IDC and lecture rooms. Gradually, staff started to use the facilities to improve their lectures, although some thought it was a good place for the graphic artist to design their wedding invitations.

We were at the top of our game in pursuing instructional design and resource-based learning. The newly appointed librarian, Peter Lor and I were asked to go and visit similar units in other parts of the world. First stop for me was Cape Town, or the Mother City, as South Africans call it. I was stunned by Cape Town's beauty with its Table Mountain backdrop and close proximity to vineyards and the Atlantic and Indian Oceans. A real jewel. We visited a hospital learning centre with similar instructional ideas to our own, and had dinner along the coast in a converted fisherman's cottage. Little did I know that sixteen years later, I would buy an apartment of my own in Cape Town.

The real progress in the construction, design and usage of resource centres was in the USA and Europe. To research, we headed to America via a stunning twenty-four-hour stopover in Rio, where we left our tickets in the hotel safe and had to make a high-speed return to fetch them. It would be thirty years before I would make a return to the beaches of Copacabana.

Upon arrival in Los Angeles, we visited the University of Irvine and then proceeded to cross the USA in an easterly direction, stopping at institutions in Boulder, Colorado, St. Cloud, Minnesota, Tallahassee and Miami, Florida, and Baltimore, Maryland. Certainly, the most impressive was the learning centre in the small university town of St. Cloud, Minnesota, although it had the worst hotel imaginable.

We based much of our future planning on the resource centre in St. Cloud. After the USA, we carried on travelling to the United Kingdom and saw much advanced thinking at the University of Brighton. The return to Bophuthatswana saw us write a report and plan for the architects to design and build a resource centre on the now busy construction site.

At one point, my colleague Derrick Nuttall and I started a hockey club for the students. This was a great experience for us all. Many of the students were astonished to see predominantly white lecturers mixing and talking with black students after lectures. This mingling was not the case in the rest of South Africa. Don't forget South Africa was at war on the borders between Namibia and Angola, and Zimbabwe and Mozambique at the time. Mahikeng, thankfully, was very peaceful.

As regards news, radio and TV information came from the state broadcaster of South Africa, the SABC. This news was heavily censored and at times seemed strange to us in Bophuthatswana, which was now legally a multiracial society. Patricia and her two children from a previous marriage, along with our new daughter Tumelo, were now living on the campus in one of the new university houses. The two elder children were very happy in local schools. Everything was going well, and the university was admitting large numbers of students by the beginning of 1983. We decided to go on holiday to Europe in July and August 1983, and visit my parents in Bristol. Tumelo would meet her grandparents for the first time. We had a great time and finished the trip by visiting New York, on our way back to South Africa. Yes, it was the long way round!

Just before we left Bristol, I received a phone call from the president's office in Bophuthatswana. They wanted to know when I would be returning to Mahikeng. Why? Exciting news: the president had decided to start a TV station to be named Bop TV and wanted me to be the head of the educational programming. Edutel, as I quickly named it. Would I accept the position? I said yes, I was interested, but they would have to get me out of the university. I heard the person on the end of the line starting to laugh. What's the problem, I asked? No problem Mr Welch, after all we do own both institutions.

We returned to Bophuthatswana and the university, since television was not quite ready for me. Luckily for me there was a gap; I had just handed in my master's thesis to the University of Witwatersrand in South Africa. Thankfully, I graduated as television started. I would not have been able to continue with my studies and run educational TV as well.

I had bought some land in Mmabatho, a suburb of Mahikeng, and got a loan to build a house: an experience I will never forget, and never repeat. I bought the materials in cash to get a big discount from the Creamery, a strange name for a building supply company! I employed a local builder and endured four months of hell as there was always something wrong on the site. No coal for the watchman to keep warm, no petrol for the motor driven saws, no cement or sand as it had been stolen the day before, a workman bitten by a snake, theft of window frames, you name it, I got assaulted by it. Anyway, I survived and moved into a beautiful home not far from the university, and the site of the nascent TV station. I was also able to help get rid of the troublesome financial officer of the university, and get a new loan through the local building society.

Late in October 1983, I finally made the move to Bop TV, and with regrets left the university behind me.

A complete TV and studio complex were under construction, but it would take three years to complete. We had a site of 'Portakabins', erected. These buildings were hot in summer, cold in winter and filled up with sand during the windy months. Don't forget we were not far from the Kalahari Desert.

We had been given the target of getting Bop TV on the air by Dec 31, 1983. To achieve this goal, we flew in from the UK an OB, or outside broadcast truck, and this became the technical centre for the station for nearly three years. We attached a small temporary studio to the truck and transmitted all our programmes from these two facilities.

Educational television in southern Africa was in its infancy at this time. Our rival, the SABC of South Africa, had only been on the air for seven years and broadcast just two channels. Very little space or time for education. I named my educational channel Edutel and looked around for inspiration in other countries. The UK and Israel had quite advanced educational TV systems at all levels, so I paid quick visits to each country. At that time, Bophuthatswana had strong business ties with Israel, through a gentleman called Shabtai Kalmanovich. This fellow set up a visit for me to visit several educational TV setups in Israel, and I came back with many ideas. I also got a bill from Shabtai for a helicopter ride over Tel Aviv! Not surprisingly, he was eventually discovered to be an

Israeli/Russian double agent, served time in an Israeli jail, and was shot in the street upon his return to Russia.

The UK, as a result of my visit, sent a British Council officer to help launch Edutel. This was to be the last of any assistance from the UK as apartheid finally closed the door on aid for many years. The French, who also became interested in the Edutel project, allowed us to purchase solar panels and equipment for rural schools without mains electricity. I also bought some educational material from Canada and the USA, but the main thrust was to produce high school material ourselves, particularly in those subjects that were difficult to teach, such as science, maths and geography. Teachers in the classrooms needed to see master teachers at work and be able to share explanatory pictures with their pupils.

Staff helped me create the materials and visit the schools to present the materials to the teachers. Some schools received the programmes over the air and some received them by tape delivery. During an unheralded visit by me to the tape-copying studio, I discovered that we had also become a porn-copying factory! I soon put a stop to this!

The president of the country, L.M. Mangope, was a tribal chief and a former teacher. So, I went to him to appeal for teachers to be seconded to my Edutel unit. He was very gracious and gave me four excellent teachers who became the bedrock of my operation. One of them eventually took over my position when I was moved to another post in the organisation. I felt very fortunate to be given a prime-time spot in the programme schedule and dreamed up a revision quiz for school leavers called 'Moving Up'. Each year, the programme ran for thirteen weeks and moved around the country. The winners of a competition got sponsored bursaries for university. The programme proved very popular and helped many kids from poor backgrounds go to university. The programme eventually ran for fourteen years — long after I had left Bop TV.

One day a gentleman appeared at my office and said he had been sent by the president, and I should give him a job. From another part of Bophuthatswana, he turned out to be a reverend who had upset his parishioners and been chased away. He said he could help me with my administration. For a long time, he gave me nothing but problems, eventually became a top poker player and left the educational side of television.

Bop TV, with its informative, educational and entertaining programmes, was proving to be a success with the viewers, but internally we had big problems, particularly with the Rhodesian/Zimbabwean staff we had taken on in various posts. The director of television was the former head of Rhodesian television; racist actions and comments abounded. Some of the key staff members had young wives who did not like Mahikeng. The result of all this instability was the disappearance of many experienced staff as they resigned and the dismissal of many of the ex-Rhodesian staff by the president. The result for me was that on Dec 24, 1984, the president's driver came to my office on the TV site and said the boss wanted to talk to me. First of all, I did not believe him, but anyway I went out to the car and there he was in shorts and tee shirt. It was summer time after all and he was on holiday. He summoned me to get into the Mercedes and sit next to him. He told me straight away he had fired the director of television, and the head of programmes had left. Would I like to run programming for Bop TV and report to him? I was a bit shocked as I thought initially he wanted to fire me as well! I said yes but I would not carry stories about the staff to him! African chiefs are notorious for wanting to hear all the gossip. He glowered at me and then laughed. That was the beginning of a great three-year relationship.

Bop TV had been on the air for just one year when I took over as head of programmes. It had given its only rival, the South African Broadcasting Corporation (SABC), a great shock. Bop TV was entertaining, informative and educational. All the things SABC was not! The SABC had started in 1976 and was, quite frankly, boring. Much propaganda, limited transmission hours, not much entertainment, and dual language broadcasts in English and Afrikaans.

As I took over BOP in late 1984, I decided to recruit new presenters, improve the on-air look, and acquire fresher and more entertaining international programmes even though my boss, the president, insisted we televised some local programme that featured Bophuthatswana and its people. And of course, the national anthem at the end of transmission every day.

My predecessor, Tim Ellis, had bravely persuaded the president to transmit the mini-series called 'Roots'. The fantastic show chronicled the story of a black American who had traced his roots back to slavery and west Africa. The series had been a huge success in America and had featured an on-screen interracial relationship. Apartheid still dominated the country, and the transmission of this show caused a sensation in the main centres of South Africa, where Bop TV could be seen. In fact, it was illegal to show such programming, and the South African government complained to my boss, the president. He ignored them, and so I continued to push back the limits of TV programming in southern Africa! One programme I did not transmit, and I now regret that decision, was called 'Tsiamelo' and it was brought to me by a wonderful lady called Ellen Khuzwayo. This documentary showed how Ellen's family had been dispossessed of their land and focused on the great persons in her family who fought the terrible injustice. Sorry, Ellen: I should have shown it, but at the time it was politically too hot to handle.

'Roving Report' was a weekly roundup of the world's news produced in London by ITV. Of course, at the time, it featured news of Mandela and the ANC movement. All banned in South Africa in 1984. I bought the programme and personally edited the show every week to ensure we pushed back against Apartheid taboos despite continued pressure from the South African government.

Four letter words and childbirth had never been heard or seen on southern African TV. So once again I bought some excellent documentaries, and one of them featured the word 'fuck'. Amazingly, no one complained after the transmission. Childbirth, a very sensitive area for black women and never to be seen by white men particularly, was shown in another documentary. The programme caused a storm of protest, especially from the president himself who told me that bare breasts in African culture were not embarrassing, but showing the other private parts was not allowed. He also told me his citizens did more than singing and dancing, and I should produce fewer local programmes featuring choirs!

Religious programming on Sundays was offered initially by local churches but the shows quickly disappeared as the church leaders all quarrelled amongst themselves. In the end, we broadcast the immensely popular shows from evangelists Jimmy Swaggart, Pat Robertson and Jerry Falwell. I travelled to Lynchburg, Virginia and met Falwell. Certainly a charismatic character, who ate a big tub of ice cream in front of me as he described the shows he could sell. All the other evangelists either paid for their shows to be aired, or gave them to us for nothing!

The big selling point for Bop TV was its entertainment shows and movies. These were mainly American action productions, comedies, animation, children's shows, documentaries and music. And eventually sport! More on it coming up! Bop TV had started with old US crime shows, such as 'Kojak' and 'Hawaii Five-O', but I quickly realised we could outgun our rivals by purchasing the very latest programmes and running them within fifteen days of their screening in the USA. The strategy yielded great publicity and brought in good commercial sales. Our audience was delighted. We also ran all two hundred and fifty-six episodes of 'M*A*S*H', which finished in February 1983 in the USA. The last episode was seen by a hundred and twenty-five million viewers in America.

'M*A*S*H', about a mobile army surgical unit in Korea, was a real eye opener for a black audience who saw army doctors being humorous while being surrounded by violent death. Later top, beloved shows included 'Hill Street Blues', a realistic cop show; 'St. Elsewhere', a superb hospital show featuring the first appearance of an AIDS story in 1983; 'Moonlighting', a sparkling romantic comedy with Bruce Willis and Cybill Shepherd; and 'The A-Team', a family action drama. The channel appealed to viewers of all ages. Not bad for a little outlet in the bush, hidden from the main road in Mahikeng, close to washing lines and shacks. This view was BBC broadcaster Michael Buerk's when he revealed Bop TV to the world!

In the 1980s, apart from live sport, all programmes were delivered on tape by air freight. Initially these tapes were one inch wide, but later reduced to three quarters of an inch. Whatever the tape size, we were dependent upon airlines and companies such as DHL to get the tapes from Johannesburg to Mahikeng, a distance of two hundred and forty kilometres. The local airport was still under construction in the early days, and so could not be used. Tapes fell off trucks and were delivered by civilians who had found them on the highway. Planes were hired to fly that evening's episode to a local airstrip where a car rushed the tape to the studio for almost instant transmission. Presenters coming from Johannesburg were instructed to pick up an outstanding tape from the airport, and I don't think we ever had to apologise for the non-transmission of a hotly awaited episode.

By the time Bop TV came on the air on Dec 31, 1983, Equity, the UK actor's union, had banned sales of programmes featuring their members to South Africa. Previously the South African Broadcasting Corporation had broadcast shows like 'The Sweeney', but this had all come to an end. The ban was commercially stupid, as southern African TV channels turned to the USA for the bulk of their programming, and English dramatic series and voices, but not movies disappeared from South Africa for about twenty years. The ban did nothing to bring down Apartheid and led to the quick Americanisation of the country. When in London, I tried to convince Equity to look favourably on lifting the ban on Bop TV, which was part of a new multiracial society. No use, they did not want to listen. However, one day, I got a phone call from Reginald B., a supposed Equity member who said he could help me. He was willing to put on a music show in London that I could use as a Christmas special. I would break the Apartheid ban!

When I met Reginald in London, we agreed the show would feature a host of London stage performers and star Danny Williams (of 'Moon River' fame) and Nina Simone. The special would be recorded at the Savoy Theatre in aid of the Kenya Heart Foundation. I returned to London for the show, had all my clothes stolen on the flight from Johannesburg and turned up at the theatre in jeans and tee shirt. Everybody else wore a dinner jacket and bowtie! The recording went well, and two days later I left for Africa with the tapes. The Christmas 1985 broadcast went smoothly with no complaints from Equity or the performers. And Reginald B. got paid. A little later he returned to Sun City in South Africa as the manager of Danny Williams! I had thought Danny was a member of Equity and the Musicians Union!

From our portable office estate and permanently attached news truck, Bop TV continued to produce great television, but there were gremlins on the horizon. Our equipment, especially microwave links and transmitters, were targeted by the South African state, and power supplies were continually interrupted. To overcome the power problem, we installed an uninterrupted power supply, or UPS, which consisted of a mammoth hut of continually hissing batteries and a large diesel generator. The theory was the batteries would continue to supply power for about three minutes if the main supply was interrupted, and then the generator would take over. One Sunday, I happened to visit the office just as the mains power cut out. The battery farm started to hiss like an angry dragon, and the generator coughed without starting. Eventually the batteries gave up, and so did the generator. There was no engineer available, so I had a look at the generator and found it was empty of diesel. Someone had pumped it dry! I drove my car to the garage next to Kentucky Fried Chicken and filled up the cans I bought. Within minutes we were back on the air.

Bop TV employed staff from many countries in the early years. Many were highly skilled and intelligent; others were willing to learn, and many others were there just for the ride. It was a multiracial environment with many wives and children on the scene — at times an explosive environment.

I began to get complaints from programme suppliers that we were not returning signed contracts to them. I could not understand. I was signing everything presented to me. I checked at the post office which confirmed they had not been sending registered letters overseas. Eventually, I found all my envelopes unsent in a cupboard in an unoccupied office. I called my assistant Trevor F. and he admitted he had been too lazy to go to the post office. He got a severe warning, and a year later during a programme purchasing trip to Monte Carlo, he collapsed dead drunk in the fountain at the then Loews Hotel! His friend and colleague J.S. also got inebriated one evening, returned to the station, and was refused entry by the security team. He retorted by racially abusing them, which led to a police arrest. I had to rescue him from the police station, and he got a severe warning.

Late one evening, I was catching up on paperwork at the office when I heard a scream and a crash. I looked out of my door and saw our training officer pursuing one of the cleaners who had been beating him with a broom. She escaped, so I ignored it. Drinking and stealing alcohol became a problem wherever we took our outside broadcast truck (by now we had two) to hotels and venues for recordings or live broadcasts.

Our first live boxing event from the famous Sun City, located in Bophuthatswana, was in 1984, when South African heavyweight Gerrie Coetzee attempted to defend his world heavyweight crown against American Greg Page. The fight was a big gig for us and we took a big crew. Unfortunately, some of them were overawed by the hotel bars, got drunk and stole liquor. Some of the stolen bottles were found in the OB truck. I fired the driver, put him in the local jail for the night and made him walk back a hundred and fifty kilometres to the studio! He begged to come back to Bop TV.

Breakdowns with overheating generators at Christmas Carol Concerts, quarrels with the army on coverage of their Independence Day tattoo, wrong lenses to film firework displays, and singers who suddenly refused to perform: all part of the happy days at Bop TV. On-air as well, new presenters panicked and had to be removed quickly. Our local staff struggled with the pronunciation of UK soccer teams, such as Norwich, Leicester, Tottenham and Southampton. The biggest mistake of all: the UK Football Association, or FA Cup. Our presenter proudly announced that next up was a 'Fuck Up'! The crew exploded with laughter, and we cut to black before bringing back the presenter who apologised, and managed to get it right, second time around.

Sport had become a potentially important part of our schedule, but programming was difficult to purchase as our rivals owned most of the local sports rights. Our research showed soccer and boxing to be two of the key sports. Satellite links from Europe and the USA were available to us, but expensive at five thousand US dollars per hour, not to mention that satellite access was then controlled by the notoriously difficult South African Post Office. Occasionally, we downlinked a boxing match from the USA without permission.

Unexpectedly, I got a call from the president's office. He said he wanted me to talk about boxing at Sun City, which was firmly part of Bophuthatswana. The president insisted that the SABC must not be allowed to transmit boxing any more from his country. Robin, throw them out, he said! The process started, and jointly SABC and Bop TV, in December 1984, produced the World Heavyweight title fight between Gerrie Coetzee and Greg Page. The event was Coetzee's only defence of the title, and he lost the fight! The event was a big success for Bop TV, and during 1985, we began covering regular fights at Sun City. Yes, I forbade the SABC to transmit from the location, or take our signal. We had a few stand-offs, and I threw their cameras out of the building on one occasion. But we won the battle.

I started commentating on air and adding to the production of the boxing shows with live cameras in the dressing room, and much scene-setting footage of helicopters over Sun City, which promoted our production, even if for a small audience. From mid-1985, Sol Kerzner, boss of the hotel group, allowed us to do all the regular tournaments. We even took boxing to other parts of Bophuthatswana, near Pretoria and Bloemfontein. Our regular meetings with the minister, now in charge of Bop TV, and one informal meeting with President Mangope made it clear we were on the right track in informing, educating and entertaining the nation. Although the cabinet always wanted to be seen on Bop TV, I had to inform them they had to do more interesting things than opening schools and water pipes.

Soccer is the number one sport for black South Africans. Once a Bophuthatswana soccer league was developed, we transmitted some of their games. International soccer was available but on a limited basis. Although the UK Premier League was only available as a taped highlight programme, the UK Football Association Cup, the FA Cup, was available for occasional live games, especially the semi-final and final. We struck a deal, and Bop TV started to show highlights and live games in 1985. At the same time, I managed to buy the European Cup Final on May 29, 1985, between Juventus and Liverpool, played in Brussels' Heysel Stadium. Juventus won the game but crowd violence resulted in thirty-nine fans dead and over six hundred injured. I watched the live pictures coming in, and was appalled by the fighting and smoke in the stands. Amazingly the game continued and for an African audience, which until then had seen little live international football, it must have been a puzzling sight to see such violence amongst white people at a sports event.

Bop TV continued to provide a refreshing change for audiences, and despite SABC efforts to block out the signal, potential viewers went to great lengths with huge aerials and dishes to see our programmes. From my time as head of educational TV, I had developed a school leavers' revision quiz called 'Moving Up'. It was normally programmed from September to mid-November to coincide with the matric, or final secondary school exam, and the key to university entrance. As an educationalist by training, I realised we could use a quiz format with teachers and potential school leavers as the stars. On the programme, we covered questions on the most difficult parts of the syllabus. The three eventual top scorers of the quiz received university bursaries from Philips Electrical. The quiz was a big success and ran for more than fourteen years. It gave bursaries to many poor students, some of whom, I am delighted to say, have reached high positions in education and industry. I later produced and featured in a short series to accompany 'Moving Up', highlighting the careers available in southern Africa.

On June 12, 1986, South Africa declared a state of emergency that covered all of South Africa, but legally not the independent homelands such as Bophuthatswana. I did not notice much change in Mahikeng, where I lived, but when travelling across South Africa to get to the various parts of Bophuthatswana, bevies of local Afrikaner farmers patrolled the streets armed with rifles. Black and white folks travelling together were viewed with suspicion! At about this time, I was in a place called Kuruman, producing an episode of the 'Moving Up' quiz. I got a message from my office, no mobile phones in those days, saying a Mr Stofberg from Johannesburg urgently wanted to speak to me. Nothing I could do for a few days until I returned to the studio in Mahikeng.

Some of the original staff from Bop TV, who had left at the end of 1984, had been recruited for what became the third pay TV operation in the world, originally named Mnet. Mr Cobus Stofberg, one of the founding executives, had been in touch with me a few months before about joining this exciting new venture. At that time there was no position for me, and they had appointed my old Bop TV friend and colleague, Tim Ellis, as head of programmes. I was still very happy at Bop TV, and my family liked Mahikeng. Everybody was worried about making a leap to Johannesburg, and big bad South Africa. Eventually I went to Jo'burg for an interview and was offered the position of deputy head of programmes, with special responsibility for the open, non-encoded slot, between six and eight p.m. each day, on-air presentation, and station look. I took leave from Bop TV, and spent several weeks incognito at Mnet. My boss at Bop TV found out anyway and tried to sack me. I joined Mnet in early August 1986 with an on-air deadline for end of October 1986. A new adventure began, and I never did move into the new Bop TV offices in Mahikeng!

South Africa at the time was engaged in a border war that would continue until 1988 and would be one of the turning points in the history and development of the continent, according to author Fred Bridgland. More than two thousand soldiers died, and there was also an internal struggle. You were aware of local security in the white areas, but it was not too hard on everyday life. Indeed, our studio buildings had no real security, apart from a guard at the gate, and could easily have been

overrun. Surprisingly, great efforts were being made at Mnet to recruit non-white staff.

Local news from the South African Broadcasting Corporation was obviously heavily censored, and events in South Africa more well known in the rest of the world. For instance, the Church Street bombing in Pretoria on May 23, 1983, which killed eight black and eleven white people hardly made any news in Bophuthatswana, where we were living at the time. We went about our business in a bubble, and rumours were rife. No doubt discussions had already commenced between the ANC and the National Party, but were kept secret as the Nats struggled to keep the lid on the pressure building both internally and externally. By 1989, South Africa's last national race-based national elections had taken place, with the ruling Nats only getting forty-eight per cent of the vote. Less than three years later, President de Klerk announced, in February 1990, that Mandela would be released after twenty-seven years in prison. In the 1992 referendum, 1.8 million of the 2.8 million white voters supported the reform of Apartheid.

Against this background, Mnet was established in South Africa and came on the air at the end of October 1986. At that time the two other existing stations were HBO in the USA and Canal Plus in France. Neither was doing particularly well, and Canal Plus only survived for a time by transmitting porn! Both these channels have since achieved great success in television history.

As a point of interest, Sky TV in the UK came on the air with four channels on Feb 5, 1989. The owners of Mnet were the South African press barons who had seen much of their income disappear after the state-owned commercial channel SABC took much of their advertising when it started in 1976. The press, which backed the Nationalist Party for the most part, went to government and demanded a business that would revitalise their interests

By chance, a young, influential Afrikaner, Koos Bekker, who had studied in America and seen HBO, returned to South Africa and convinced the newspaper owners that pay TV was the answer and could be very lucrative. Government was approached by the press group, and President Botha and his cabinet licensed the company now known as Media24. There had been other potential bidders including Sol Kerzner, of Sun International Hotels fame, but these were brushed aside in favour of the press group. No news was to be allowed on the fledgling channel so that government could control propaganda, and each newspaper had to invest according to their size and circulation. Koos Bekker and two of his college friends, Cobus Stofberg and Jacques van de Merwe (later killed in a plane crash in the French Alps), were to be the driving force behind the station.

I had done a good job at Bop TV, turning it into a commercial success and an enjoyable station to watch. But as anti-Apartheid pressure built, and programming became harder to purchase, it was useful having an

English passport holder on board who could travel without hindrance. No doubt this was another plus point counting towards my appointment at Mnet. The founders were so called enlightened Afrikaners who realised that the country had to change and understood my predicament, coming to live in South Africa with a black wife and children. They undertook to resolve my situation and get me a permit to live in a white area, since I refused to live in Soweto. The permit took nearly three years to obtain. I still have it and remember the many threats to deport me. Usually on a Friday afternoon!

Initially, I lived with the children in a multiracial hotel, or friends' homes, until I was able to buy a home in Randburg, a suburb of Johannesburg. The kids were admitted to a multiracial private school and having sold our house in Mahikeng, my wife moved down to Jo'burg. Occasionally, as an illegal mixed couple, we would be insulted on the street and get offensive phone calls. But we survived and found a great deal of goodwill amongst friends and colleagues.

Against this difficult political, economic, and personal background we battled to set up the pay TV station. We moved offices constantly, struggling to establish our studios, transmission headquarters, administration, decoder sales offices, and phone-in departments. New clients were particularly reluctant to sign up for this new so-called video operator! At this time, video stores were rampant in South Africa and full of pirated material.

The initial investment from the newspapers was soon exhausted, and more funds were needed. Subscribers, advertisers, sponsors and suppliers of movies were all difficult to find. Companies were suspicious and in the case of movies and sport we found our rivals, SABC had bought everything in advance, or Apartheid meant suppliers were banned from dealing with us.

The founders of the company originally envisaged Mnet to be a movie only channel with a few kids' programmes and occasional documentaries sprinkled in. Of course, we had our 'open time' to encourage viewers to join up with the complete channel, and enjoy all the movies and occasional events. Open time lasted for two hours every evening and played mainly American series and later on soaps, such as 'Loving'. This was our shop window. You did not need a decoder to watch, and we hoped you would be tempted to take the plunge and subscribe to the complete channel. Meanwhile, my experience as a sportsman, and an executive at Bop TV, and my upbringing in UK, where I had seen television since 1959, convinced me that we had to get into sport.

Local sport, such as cricket and rugby, was in the hands of the SABC, and much overseas sport was not available to us. However, two sports, boxing and golf were accessible locally and internationally. The latter

came mainly through the success of Gary Player, who hailed from South Africa. I managed to persuade the three wise men at the helm of the company to try one boxing tournament, which our American consultant in Los Angeles was also transmitting on his channel. This turned out to be one of the fights of the century, and we paid fifty thousand US dollars for the rights.

The fight we wanted was Marvin Hagler vs. Sugar Ray Leonard on April 6, 1987. Leonard had returned after a long absence from the ring and 'Marvelous' Marvin Hagler, a great champion, was expected to deal with him easily. I did not go to bed because I wanted to watch the fight broadcast from Las Vegas in the early hours of the morning. Our marketing department had assembled groups of guests in various cinemas and halls throughout Johannesburg, and we assembled terrific marketing in the newspapers. We really hoped to make our presence felt in what was after all only seven months since we had launched the channel in October 1986. Satellite transmissions in those days were still unreliable and susceptible to storms, sunspots, etc. and I had a feeling that we might have a problem. As insurance I booked London Weekend TV in the UK to provide me with a secondary feed, including pictures and commentary.

Sure enough as we crossed to ringside, we had a picture but no sound. Unknown to me much of the world was also without sound. To this day no one knows why! I asked my satellite engineer to bring in the London

Weekend TV signal, and miraculously they had their own separate commentary feed, so we were able to patch that into our picture.

Guests in the theatres clapped when they realised what had happened. The show had been saved, and we received great publicity for the channel. We also witnessed a great fight, the result of which has been disputed ever since. The bosses were delighted, and suddenly subscriptions began selling.

Boxing had worked so well, I then tied up boxing output deals with some of the world's great promoters such as Bob Arum, Cedric Kushner, Mickey Duff and Dan Duva. Suddenly, we had a feast of live boxing featuring the world's greatest. Subscribers loved it. Keeping the momentum going, we looked at local boxers who we thought would give even more local flavour to the viewers. The first fighter we chose was called Brian Mitchell. He was a gem. He had just won the WBA Junior Lightweight title at Sun City, Bophuthatswana on September 27, 1986. He went on to defend his title twelve times and retired undefeated in September 1991. Apartheid bans meant he could never defend his title in South Africa, so he was always on the road. A fantastic achievement.

After being unhappy with our boxing presentation and commentary for some time, I went on air as one of the commentators and redesigned the total boxing show experience. More cameras, punch counts, shots in the dressing room, pre- and post-match interviews, features of the boxers at home and in training, features on the venues and countries, and so on. Viewers loved it and looked forward to their regular appointment with the show. These were great times for South African boxing and fighters such as Johnny Du Plooy, Harold Volbrecht, Welcome Ncita, and Pierre Coetzer.

Road trips around the world with fighters were eventful and fun. When Brian Mitchell fought in France in October 1987, we had to start the fight without the promoter's permission because he insisted on changing the timings. I simply told the referee to get on with it since we were paying the champion. The promoter exploded. Brian's title defence in Spain against José Rivera in April 1988 nearly did not happen because Spain had just been awarded the Barcelona Olympic Games that day. The promoter was told by Spanish National TV not to cover the fight with a South African for fear of endangering the Olympics decision. Eventually I pushed both fighters into the ring and got on with it. Mitchell's defence in London against Jim McDonnell in November 1988 was nearly halted by anti-Apartheid demonstrators. Promoter Mickey Duff got a court order, and the fight continued with a mainly black audience, including heavyweight Frank Bruno. We left the auditorium by the back door, helped by the police. The BBC's great boxing commentator, Harry Carpenter, worked next to me that night.

When Brian Mitchell took on Salvatore Bottiglieri in Capo D'Orlando, Italy in February 1989, Afrikaans commentator Retief Uys thought the shower caps were condoms. Later in 1989, during Mitchell's defence against Jackie Beard, Cedric Kushner put up the wrong sponsors banner, and the Italian promoter wanted more money to authorise my satellite link. I agreed to the increase, but of course never paid him! Fights in the USA were always difficult, with potential anti-Apartheid demonstrators, and in Lewiston, Maine in September 1989, a crowd did appear, but was chased away by the local woodchoppers, who wanted to see the fight. Brian's last fight in Sacramento USA against Tony Lopez in September 1991 was a rough but not sparkling match, which was enlivened at the closing press conference by the fighters two wives who threw punches at each other until separated by the stewards.

Johnny du Plooy was a South African heavyweight who fought for a world title in Italy in May 1989 and lost. During the fight, commentated by ITV's Reg Gutteridge and myself, my seat broke and I ended up on the floor next to ringside. Two ladies in the audience sprang forward, dusted me down and put me back in my chair. Reg never stopped pulling my leg about how quickly I could chat up women.

Working on world title fights meant I met some of the great boxing trainers and cornermen, including Emmanuel Steward from Chicago, who handled some of the great fighters of the eighties and nineties and a phenomenal cutman called Chuck. Chuck was a staunch Catholic who loved visiting European cathedrals with me, and when we were promoting in Europe, my job was to take him to as many cathedrals as possible so he could pray. Chuck regretted that his only son did not want to learn the cutman's secrets, which are usually passed from father to son. Chuck told me he earned fifty thousand US dollars per fight, and was given absolute control over wounded fighters. He worked with many top fighters including Evander Holyfield. The secret to prevent cuts and bleeding during a fight, according to Chuck, was the preparation of the boxer's face with various potions in the weeks leading up to the event. He refused to tell me the ingredients of his magic potions!

Boxing produces some extraordinary champions, and one such was Roberto Duran (world middleweight champ). I met him in Panama City in 1989 along with his legendary manager, Luis Spada, who handled the second half of Roberto's glittering career. From very humble beginnings, he amassed and lost a fortune. I tried to interview him, but his English was poor, and so I pulled him closer to the mike. His body really was like his hands — reputed to be made of stone. A rock of a man! A great character.

In the same year, sitting in an airport lounge somewhere in the USA, I met another boxing legend called Bruce 'The Mouse' Strauss. He said he could fight at any weight apart from heavyweight. The mouse tricked the scales to show lighter weights, added lead to his boots to increase his weight, and fought all over the USA and abroad as a journeyman available at a moment's notice at just about any weight required by the promoter or tournament. Bruce, whose life was recounted in an HBO movie, loved boxing, knew he would never be a champion and became a firm favourite with crowds as a good opponent.

Besides boxing and golf, we realised we had to produce events of our own. Local rugby was owned by our rivals, so we invented an annual North vs. South rugby game in South Africa. The best players from the north of the country versus the pick of the south. This programming brought us to the attention of the BBC, which had the worldwide rights to Five Nations Rugby at the time.

We decided to buy the package, but the Irish Rugby Union objected to their games being televised in South Africa. I phoned the head of sport at Irish State TV and remonstrated with him in a gentle but firm manner. Suddenly he said we could televise the games as my name Welch was part Irish, and he liked my voice. I guaranteed him Guinness and lunch next time I was in Dublin, and the deal was done.

The BBC was astonished, and granted us satellite permission to transmit the Irish games. About the same time, a sponsor suggested we organise an ultra-marathon (fifty-seven kilometres) in South Africa. This rare event attracted older athletes from around the world who did not worry about South African politics. The ultra was run around the town of Stellenbosch and the winelands of South Africa. It was a big production with many outside broadcast trucks and helicopters. A terrific production for South Africa at the time. I even did some of the commentary myself, and a local genius called Ray Wilson, assisted by Mark Williams, directed the event. A local runner called Bruce Fordyce collapsed at my feet as I was interviewing him. Many years later he told me he could not speak, he was totally... The runners spread all over the course, and I closed down the transmission about one hour after Bruce was declared the winner. Fellow executives and relatives of the runners castigated me for this because they wanted to see the remaining athletes. However, the transmission was becoming boring with some athletes still two hours from the finish. The race has never been run in South Africa again, and is rarely seen in other parts of the world.

Besides sport, I controlled, or at least tried to control, the on-air presenters and put up with their crises and demands for hairdos and clothes. Many on air mistakes were made, and some presenters, without my knowledge, recorded their links so they could go home early. One evening, the transmission producer illegally entertained his girlfriend outside the studio. The presenter had left her recorded link, and the computer failed to cue it to the next programme. Result: we went to black, a terrible crime in television. The station switchboard glowed red hot, irate bosses phoned me, and I rushed to the studio to sort out the mess. The producer, who was still dallying with his girlfriend, did not realise what had happened!

Working an eighty-hour week, my duties also included local production. I successfully produced 'Holiday on Ice' at Sun City with a marvellous Canadian cast that taught my presenter to skate in thirty minutes. Next up, also at Sun City in 1987, was a show with the German pop group Modern Talking, who were very big worldwide at the time. The lead singer Thomas Anders was a great performer and decent person. His blonde girlfriend, who insisted on being part of the group, was very difficult and domineering. The deal for our station was to carry their last show almost live on a Saturday night. TV show director Ray Wilson and I decided to record the Friday night show as a rehearsal. Luckily!

About five thousand fans packed into the Sun City auditorium on the Saturday night. I was backstage, and Ray was happily directing the show when a note arrived from the lady in the band saying if we did not close our cameras, she would push one of the cameramen off the stage into the audience: a drop of about two metres. I told Ray to shut down, except for the wide shot of the complete band. The lady seemed happy with this and we got to the end of the concert. The wannabe dominatrix did not know that as she walked off stage, we ran our recorded tape of the Friday night's concert for our viewers. Folks at home did not know about the drama we faced. Within ten minutes, the lady member of

Modern Talking attacked me in the dressing room with an ice bucket. Both of us had to be restrained by security. I refused to pay Modern Talking, who wanted cash, and we made sure their concerts in Cape Town were poorly attended. So came to an end my period of local production, but not before I had produced 'The Rozanne Botha Show' with the daughter of the state president, and a new man arrived.

Meanwhile my stewardship of open time viewing continued, and I made several trips to the European TV festivals and also to Hollywood to buy programming. I was invited by Warner Brothers to a party at the Playboy Mansion in the Hollywood Hills. I enjoyed a lift in a Rolls Royce from the movie buyer of Irish TV, who looked just like Alfred Hitchcock and had his plain-looking daughter with him. The mansion was loaded with Hefner's latest girlfriends with whom I had some interesting conversations. I went for a walk in the gardens and found the underground grotto which asked guests not to piss in the pool! After plenty of champagne, I tried to get a lift with the Dutch movie buyer. But her car would not start. So, we had the embarrassing incident of push-starting her small compact American car down the drive of one of America's most well-known homes.

On duty one evening in March 1987, I received a phone call from my father informing me my mother had passed away. She had been cured of breast cancer a few years earlier and died from a heart attack whilst ironing a shirt for my dad. They had been together for nearly fifty years and Dad was heartbroken. I flew back to the UK next day, and we cremated her a few days later in Bristol. Family and friends gathered, but I was astonished to see how little I had in common with all of them. I had been away from UK for eleven years and my thoughts and feelings were so different from theirs. Many of them were little Englanders who had never left the UK, and thought I was mad to live in an African country that looked to be on the edge of revolution. I don't think they understood the sunshine and excitement and challenges of Africa.

My contract manager at the time was an Indian South African called Ron Moodley. We became good friends and remained so until his death in 2008. During the early days of Mnet, the company would provide drinks for the staff on a Friday afternoon. For nearly one year we ran the whole company with only thirty people, and we all did weeks of eighty hours or more. Free drinks were a nice gift for the hard-pressed staff. The liquor policy had to come to an end as eventually staff numbers escalated to about ninety, and management could not afford the bill. Ron and I decided to visit the local pub on a Friday afternoon, but I had forgotten that Apartheid rules forbade non-white persons to visit bars and restaurants unless the owners had obtained a special licence. So began our journey to find a multiracial pub in South Africa. Not easy! Despite many rude refusals and threats to our safety, we persisted until we found a pleasant and welcoming waterhole. Ron never forgot this new chapter in his life, and later on we visited India together. Despite his Indian origins, Ron always remained suspicious of his country, and during his first trip told me he was frightened to leave the hotel. On the phone I said don't be frightened, you look like one of them!

Looking back, having started many TV channels throughout the world, I realise that the best times are usually the first three or four years before the accountants get their hands on the budget. This rule was certainly true at Mnet and so the fun continued. We desperately needed new sports content, and my interest in cycling, and having lived in France, led me to the Tour de France in June 1987. I contacted the owners one evening at a hotel in Pau. They were astonished that I could speak French and readily agreed on a deal for the 1987 Tour. We would take daily highlights and on the final day from Paris, go live. Our sponsorship manager, Kate Monaghan, soon found a sponsor and since 1987, the Tour de France has been a regular fixture on the winter schedule of DSTV, as it is now called. Worried that we would lose the audio track to the live final race day, I flew to Paris and set up a landline in a hotel and was ready to take on the commentary if necessary. Luckily all went well and Irishman Stephen Roche won the race without my assistance.

The first World Rugby cup event was held in New Zealand in June 1987. South Africa was banned, but there was great interest in the event, especially since a South African rugby team had toured New Zealand illegally in the 1980s. Our management wanted a coup after the Hagler/Leonard fight in April 1987— one that would entice more subscribers. I suggested we could, at a price, get the Rugby World Cup final, so I set up a deal to download and record the event in London, then bring the tape back to Johannesburg. I flew to London one Friday night, recorded the game live from New Zealand as it came in early on the Saturday morning, and set off back to Heathrow for the flight that Saturday night. Publicity had been prepared, and as soon as I was on the flight, the secret news was released. Watch the World Cup Final on Mnet this Sunday evening. The screening caused a sensation and encouraged more new subscribers to join the service as we pushed harder and harder to reach the magic total of three hundred thousand subscribers: break-even point! Later on, I used the same technique to show the Commonwealth Games from New Zealand in 1990. Tapes were again recorded in London and shipped every night by air to Johannesburg via Lesotho, the latter being a recognised Commonwealth country where anti-Apartheid rules did not apply.

A non-sporting incident occurred in mid-1987, when I took a phone call from a lecturer at the University of the Witwatersrand in Johannesburg. He said he was from the department of agriculture and wanted to talk about my experiences in

Bophuthatswana. I met him for lunch in a well-known restaurant in Johannesburg where he immediately said he knew a lot about me and former ministers in Bophuthatswana. He asked me pertinent questions about these persons, including informing me that at least one of my former ministers had died in a faulty vehicle 'accident'. He mentioned another acquaintance by name and said the British government wanted him back in the UK on charges of fraud in Zambia and now in Bophuthatswana. This gentleman had no business in Africa! Needless to say, he was an MI6 agent who wanted to recruit me to work in southern Africa. I refused and left the restaurant. About one year later, this fellow produced a book on agriculture in Bophuthatswana and promptly left the University of Witwatersrand and South Africa.

Despite Apartheid, many celebrities continued to visit the country. Society hostess Viviane Ventura brought out Ursula Andress and Britt Ekland for one of our programme launch parties. Both were charming and recounted many interesting stories. Ursula Andress, after all, was in the first James Bond movie, 'Dr No', emerging from the ocean in her tight, wet swimsuit, armed with a knife.

Stan Matthews, later Sir Stanley Matthews, the great footballer, was a regular winter visitor to South Africa for more than twenty years and held soccer coaching clinics for black kids in Soweto. He also analysed soccer games on screen for me in the early days of our TV sport shows. Always wanted to be paid as soon as he finished the show and told me he should have played until he was sixty, and not fifty! Even then, he knew about bribery in soccer and envelopes being handed over at motorway cafés in the UK.

Stan's Wednesday lunches in Johannesburg were legendary. He always ate fish and chips, washed down with soft drinks. Stan was a teetotaller all his life and would not have beer or wine on the table. The great footballer's sponsors also brought out to South Africa some of Matthews' 1953 Cup Final team: Stan Mortenson, Bill Perry, Jackie Mudie and this time, much to Stan's disgust, alcohol got served with dinner! Stan's son, Stan Matthews junior, was a top tennis player and lived in America where he established tennis clinics. Stan was proud of him and of his daughter, who lived in northern South Africa after marrying the manager of a cement plant. Stan visited her from time to time and was always astonished by the rugged beauty of the country. Eventually, Stan went back to the UK and no longer wintered in South Africa. Meanwhile, Gary Bailey, the Manchester United and England goalkeeper, returned to South Africa where he was born, and became our leading soccer commentator. For several years we had taken the First Division highlights from the UK on tape on a Wednesday evening. Live games were not available. Then in 1989, we could contract for live First Division Games. I rushed to London to see the agents CSI and managed to outbid our rivals, the South African Broadcasting Corporation, with a princely sum of one million US dollars for a three-year deal and the possibility of two games per week.

Upon my arrival at the headquarters of CSI in London, the owner Michael Watt refused to see me because he claimed I had been rude to his secretary. Untrue! He then softened his approach and let me into his office as long as I promised to watch his horses running in a televised race meeting. Michael was a pugnacious New Zealander who had managed Lester Piggott the top UK jockey, and had also been clerk of the racecourse in York. Horses were of great interest to him.

As the TV programme finished, Michael turned to me and said what the f*** do you want? I told him I had come for the f****** UK soccer. We engaged in a long harangue and kind of agreed on a package of sport including live games via satellite of the UK First Division. Michael said he was in a hurry and asked me what I was doing that evening. I told him I was going to see Dad, who was still alive and well in Bristol. Typical Michael, all bluster and generosity, gave me his car and driver to drive to Bristol for the evening. Michael Watt, who always supported the underdog, financed the Durham Miners Gala in UK on several occasions, and in my presence gave air tickets to families who wanted to visit relatives overseas. He now owns part of Ronnie Scott's Jazz Club in London and is a financier for new stage plays in the West End. A good-hearted pioneer of the business! We eventually settled the soccer deal when Michael phoned me from Italy about a week later. I knew then we had established one of the cornerstones of the company. A must have for many viewers. Not satisfied with the First Division, which later became the Premier League in 1992. I pressed on and purchased the UK FA Cup and on April 15, 1989, witnessed live the Liverpool vs. Nottingham Forest semi-final which became the Hillsborough disaster, when many Liverpool fans died in the overcrowded stadium.

I was in the control room and saw the chaos on the pitch coming in live until eventually the game stopped. We put on a filler programme as our switchboard exploded and irate fans demanded to see more carnage. A shocking and moving experience for me.

I telephoned Peter di Palma, the then TV manager for the FA and asked him to record the other semi-final between Everton and Norwich, which was due to start forty-five minutes after our abandoned game. Peter agreed, and we started to play the second game from the point where the abandoned game would have reached halftime. Our viewers saw the second semi-final delayed, but in entirety. A few viewers phoned to congratulate my quick thinking.

Boxing continued to do well for us but not without its off-camera incidents. My experienced lead commentator was a recovering alcoholic who lapsed from time to time! In Berlin, three hours before a fight and having visited East Berlin, the land of peasants and farmers, for the last time, my co-commentator was nowhere to be seen. Eventually we broke into his room and found him very drunk. A few slaps and pots of black coffee got him into a reasonable state, and he managed two hours on air before falling asleep as the fight finished. On top of that our fighter lost.

I was still handling the open-air time series and comedies and one of them got me into trouble. The series was called 'Married with Children' and was a massive hit in the USA. I went to meet one of my bosses at a local airport for a charter flight to Lesotho. He was standing by the plane waiting for me as I walked across the tarmac and said, "Robin, we are in trouble. Viewers are complaining that yesterday Jesus Christ crashed into the backyard of a house in the USA." South Africa is a strongly religious country and people were offended. The script of 'Married with Children' was often vulgar and irreligious, and in one of the episodes, the lead actor had implied the Jesus scenario. I had to take the whole series off at the time and eventually rescheduled it about one year later. Probably the nearest I have come to the sack!

Coming towards the end of the eighties in South Africa, my black wife Pat and children were feeling more comfortable as Apartheid was coming to an end, and there were rumours about Mandela's release. However, the system still hit back at me as I was finally granted, on May 16 1989, a permit for me and my black family to live in a white area known as Blairgowrie, Johannesburg. We had already been living in the country for nearly three years, and the wheels had turned very slowly. No doubt the authorities had wanted to ignore us for as long as possible, but in the end had to obey the law. We received a few phone calls from outraged locals. I usually told them to bugger off. There was no hostility in the streets or shops although the stares abounded.

Sports negotiations were always tenuous and protracted, particularly with companies who were still suspicious of the upstart pay TV company. This was the case with a company called IMG from the USA, started by a genius called Mark McCormack, who was one of the first people to realise you could build a company around sports stars and include events and venues as part of the deal. Mark signed up the three major golf players of the sixties and seventies, namely Gary Player, Arnold Palmer and Jack Nicklaus. His hold on golf began. He went on to spread his influence to include athletics, tennis and major American sports.

The IMG representative for South Africa was the aptly named Buzz Hornett. Mr Hornett had done very little business with us, preferring to remain with his old favourite, the South African Broadcasting Corporation. One of the senior directors at Mnet suggested we invite Buzz to meet us at a game reserve. He felt Buzz would be more relaxed, and amenable to doing more and new deals with us. A superb game lodge in the Kruger Park was booked for all of us including our wives. Little did Buzz know that the conference centre at this game lodge was a tree house. My boss, Cobus Stofberg, decided to keep Buzz marooned in the tree house until he gave in and signed the exclusive rights with us for the British Open golf and Wimbledon tennis. The trick worked, and by five p.m. Buzz was desperate for a beer and a sandwich since we had not provided any lunch. He was ready to sign anything. Talk about starving a man into submission!

By late 1989, the company was doing well and had passed the magical three hundred thousand subscriber target. Three years of losses turned into profits. No more anxious looks, but smiles on many faces. At the same time, one of our programme suppliers called Daro, based in Monaco, came knocking on my door asking if I wanted to join them. They had approached me before, but I had always turned them away as I wanted to stay in Africa.

Politically, South Africa was a in a state of transition: rumours of the release of Mandela, great pressure from Europe for Apartheid to end. The family and I decided to accept the offer and live in Monaco. It took about twelve months for all the papers to be processed, and so I carried on working at Mnet as head of sport. There were still fights featuring our great boxers Brian Mitchell, Johnny du Plooy and Welcome Ncita, the latter winning his IBF Super Bantamweight Title in Tel Aviv, Israel. A world title fight in Israel was a rare event, and it marked my last big event as an employee of Mnet before we left for Monaco.

We sold our house in Blairgowrie without difficulty in March 1990, watched the truck drive away with all of our goods bound for Marseille, and moved into a hotel for a few days before the flight to the south of France. A new European life was beginning, but Africa would not be forgotten! And then there was Maud.

Arriving in Monaco, we soon settled into a comfortable flat in a suburb of Monte Carlo. Monaco covers an area of 2.02 square kilometres or 0.78 square miles, and has a very different atmosphere from Johannesburg, with yacht-lined harbours, graceful streets and homes, casinos, an elegant opera house, and many top-class hotels and restaurants. It is a hilly location with many luxury public lifts for its elderly, wealthy residents! The huge police force means that crime is very rare in Monaco and the streets are safe at all hours. The banks had no currency restrictions, unlike South Africa at the time. The two girls, after a false start, settled into the International School of Nice and my father, then seventy-six years old, came to visit us from UK. Unfortunately, my second wife Pat was having problems adjusting to the new Monégasque life. Fortunately, before I left Johannesburg I had met Maud, a top-class journalist in South Africa, who was eventually to come and join me. Frankly, my thoughts were sometimes elsewhere!

My new job was to buy and sell television programmes in Africa, Scandinavia and Portugal. Don't know how I ended up with the last two areas! Anyway, the company Daro was doing well as television companies were springing up throughout the world with the digital revolution yet to come. If I did well, I had been promised ten per cent of the company. The office was mainly staffed by ladies, and during the early months I had a succession of secretaries whose English was hopeless. Eventually I found Suzanne from the UK who had come to Monaco with her husband, a captain on a private yacht. Besides the owner and myself, there was one other gentleman called Laurent. He was the first person I had met who admitted to having AIDS! He worked hard, but after three years returned to his parents in Paris and passed away. A sad time.

My first trip back to South Africa as a salesperson, marketing television programmes, was strange as I was now on the other side of the fence and selling to former colleagues and acquaintances. It was difficult at first but I took care not to force programming onto my clients, and at the same time swallowed the jealousy of former friends in South Africa who thought I had escaped to a great place.

Until 1990, besides South Africa I had only visited three other African states: Botswana, Swaziland and Zimbabwe. From now on, I would travel constantly in Africa and eventually would visit about eighty percent of the continent. Ethiopia, with a population of over a hundred million people, very few of them white, was the first country I visited. Ethiopian Airlines and Addis Ababa were and are stunning. Addis is the commercial and cultural hub of the country, filled with handsome men and beautiful women. No doubt Africa's most stunning race.

My first visit to Addis was in late 1990, as the Ethiopian People's Revolutionary Democratic Front (EPRDF), a coalition of rebel groups, overthrew the Marxist-Leninist Derg, in power since 1974. The main square in Addis was in turmoil. Big panels showing revolutionary leaders were removed and replaced by the EPRDF. The head of television was a lady, a former actress, and she and her deputy took me out for a traditional Ethiopian meal. We all sat on the floor around a large plate of injera, or sourdough flatbread, served with vegetables and a spicy meat stew. We all ate from the same dish and tore off pieces of injera, which we used to scoop up our stew and vegetables. Delicious! At the end of the meal, my host, the lady, told me that as the guest I should eat the remaining food from her hands! Unusual but sensual!

I visited Ethiopia several times, but limited budget meant that sales were poor. From Addis I flew south, on my way to Djibouti, but on the way, I changed planes in a town in southern Ethiopia called Dire Dawa. This is Ethiopia's second city, and has a colonial quarter, Kezira, which has wide streets and a railway station dating from the French development of the railway. I did not spend much time at the airport but noticed a Yugoslav Airline Boeing 737 parked near the airport building. I asked a local person what a Yugoslav plane was doing in such a small place, and replied that it was bringing the daily supply of khat, a plant amphetamine-like stimulant chewed by the locals! I was to come across more of these magical green leaves at my next stop, Djibouti.

Djibouti, on the Horn of Africa, is a mostly French and Arabic-speaking country. Occasionally their representatives visited the television programme markets in France, so a sales visit as part of longer African trip was possible. The first problem was that I always seemed to arrive at Ramadan, when it was impossible to see Djibouti TV representatives before the sun had gone down! Secondly it always seemed to be an expensive place to visit. In reality it was still very French. The French Foreign Legion was based there, and fresh cheese and flowers were flown in daily from Paris. The local French baker was excellent. But business was small and so visits became infrequent.

The daily Air France flight from Paris stopped at Djibouti and then went onto Reunion Island. I took the flight to this French province, or department in the Indian Ocean, famous for its rainforests, active volcano and coral reefs and beaches. Reunion is truly a little bit of France, thirteen hours from Paris. Excellent roads and infrastructure. Unlike my next stop, Mauritius, an independent country with poor roads and facilities in the early 1990s. My friends in Reunion used to say, when you see Mauritius, that's why we want to remain part of France! In the 1990s, ethnically mixed Mauritius was politically unstable, and one day my contact, the head of TV programmes, was fired along with her husband the chief justice. As a result, sales plummeted and took some years to recover. During another trip to Mauritius, I hired a car from the airport in the south of the island, and as I drove north to my hotel was astonished to see only candle lights in houses and traffic lights extinguished. Unknown to me there was a general strike that day and the electricity company had shut down.

Usually from Mauritius I flew on to the Seychelles, an archipelago of a hundred and fifteen islands in the Indian Ocean. My contact was a beautiful Creole lady based in the capital, Victoria. She was always happy to have lunch with me at the TV festivals in France, but on home territory she seemed extremely nervous to meet up. Only later did I discover she was the girlfriend of a senior politician in the Seychelles. The islands were an idyllic place to visit with a frightening airport laid out alongside the coast. On one of my visits, my office phoned me, saying one of my football clients was actually offshore on one of his yachts and wanted to do a deal. I never met him but a deal was done telephonically via landline.

From the Seychelles there were occasional flights to Nairobi, Kenya, a distance of about fifteen hundred kilometres. In the early nineties, the state broadcaster

KBC had a new rival in the independent KTN, and business was booming. On one visit I arranged for Maud to join me in Nairobi. Because my flight from the Seychelles was severely delayed, it was nightfall before we met up at the airport. We hailed a black taxi, formerly a London cab, and set off for town. After about fifteen minutes, the driver informed us he had no money to buy petrol, and suddenly the cab came to a standstill. Maud thought we were going to be hijacked! Within minutes, our driver stopped another passing cab, put all of our luggage in it, jumped in and accompanied us to the Norfolk Hotel. There he demanded his fare for his part of the trip, as well as the money for the second cab!

Besides making three or four trips a year on my African circuit, I was still doing boxing commentary for Mnet back in South Africa. My last fight was covering Brian Mitchell versus Toney Lopez for the WBA/IBF Super Featherweight Championship in Sacramento, California on September 13, 1991. Mitchell, who fought twelve world title defences on the road, proved himself a true warrior that night and reunited both titles. Perhaps the best fight was between the wives of Mitchell and Lopez at the post-fight press conference. They had a real rough and tumble and had to be separated by the two boxers.

Daro, the company I represented, had done little business in west Africa, and having met representatives from many west African countries at the TV festivals, I decided to make a trip. First stop was the Cape Verde

Islands, a nation made up of ten isles floating in the Atlantic Ocean, five hundred kilometres off the coast of Senegal. In the early 1990s, Sal Island had an enormous runway built by the South Africans to enable their aircraft to land and refuel and continue to London or New York. At this time, South African Airways was banned from flying across black Africa, and badly needed a staging post. Maud and I flew from London to Sal Island and spent the night in a quaint hotel near the airport. Next day, under the command of the first lady pilot I had ever seen, we flew in a tiny box-like aeroplane to Praia, the capital on Santiago Island. Our TV hosts met us and showed us around this dilapidated former Portuguese capital where our hotel had a cracked swimming pool with no water. I did some business, and a trip around the island revealed great beaches and often desolate hills. The locals were catching some of the biggest fish I had ever seen.

A short flight from Praia took us to Dakar in Senegal, a French-speaking former colony with links to the slave trade through Goree Islands, and a magnificent first president in the poet philosopher Leopold Senghor. There were also many Lebanese traders and shopkeepers who wanted to buy my programmes and sell them to the local TV station. Next stop was the Ivory Coast and Abidjan. My friend Maud had to hand over her passport at immigration to avoid the official ban on South Africans visiting the country. She retrieved it when we left.

A magnificent highway into town greets the traveller with excellent hotels and an ice-skating rink. I presume it still exists. The Ivory Coast produces some of the best cocoa in the world, and the first drink in the morning is hot chocolate and not coffee! My TV hosts invited me to supper in the bush. I thought we would be leaving town, but in reality, it was a trip downtown to traditional restaurants where men could escape from their wives. Senegal was the only country where the customs officers wanted me to pay duty on my demonstration tapes. Needless to say, I did not.

From the relative calm of the Ivory Coast I flew onto Africa's biggest country, Nigeria, leaving Maud with her friend, the Canadian ambassador, in Abidjan. What an experience to arrive in Lagos! I was to come here regularly until 2003 when I produced the All-Africa Games in Abuja. On my flight was an American nurse sent on a training mission to a hospital in Lagos. She told me that she had heard that everybody wanted bribes in Nigeria, including customs and immigration. She, as an American, would refuse to pay them!

I passed through immigration with difficulty as my visa was deemed out of date, having been issued the day before in London. In customs, I encountered the American nurse who had said she had nothing to declare. The agent opened her case and threw all her clothes, including bras and panties, onto the table. She was humiliated and burst into tears. Eventually we met up as we were staying at the same hotel on Victoria

Island. Both of us found that our hotel reservations could not be found without rewarding the check-in clerk! I encountered many other similar occurrences in Nigeria during my visits over the next eight or so years. You could transact TV sales with both the private companies that had started in the 1990s, but not as yet Nollywood, or the Nigerian state broadcaster, NTA. I enjoyed an amusing incident with the head of NTA and her husband, at that time the ombudsman for Nigeria, in a Lagos restaurant. Refusing to accept the poor service and food, he stood up and said the staff and restaurant were a disgrace to the image of Nigeria. As the only white man in the restaurant, I nearly crept under the table!

My last visit to Nigeria was for the All-Africa Games in Abuja, Nigeria in 2003. I was the salesperson for this event, in effect the African Olympic Games. I also became the technical director, responsible for planning each day's TV coverage and downlinking all the signals coming in from the various stadia and parts of Nigeria. Many of the participating countries paid in cash for their TV coverage, and those who had not paid tried to steal the satellite signal. The thieving was soon stopped! What was not stopped was the emergence without warning of malaria in Abuja. Unfortunately, several participating athletes died.

I also visited Gabon, which had two TV stations, one of which was under the control of President Omar Bongo and involved walking with an escort carrying a machine gun and paying for a pee at the airport. Next door was Angola where I was held in prison for twelve hours and deported because allegedly my visa was incorrect. Prison was not nice, particularly the mouldy bread I was given to eat.

Zimbabwe was a good client and bought many programmes, but seemed short of car parts as I was often asked to bring clutches and brake linings for Land Rovers and Minis. Uganda gave change in huge piles of cash, and banks gave guarantees that bounced. The Namibians took me to a game reserve with pet cheetahs you could touch. Anything for a deal I suppose! Swaziland had TV staff dressed in tribal dress who would carry messages across the country, demanding to be fed if they came to your room or house.

In North Africa, we were starting to do business in Tunisia, Morocco and Algeria. The latter is a fascinating country of great potential, but hard to visit on business, particularly television, which is regarded with some suspicion. I was met by plain clothes police in Algiers who questioned me and then kindly took me to my hotel. Next day I met my contact at the state TV station — welcomed by machine guns and confiscation of my passport. My contact was unable to come and see me for dinner as Algiers was under curfew. I saw many young people and was warned not to visit the casbah because foreigners were being attacked. Algeria is the tenth largest country in the world.

Besides visiting clients in Africa and later Portugal and Scandinavia, I attended the TV conventions or conferences in Cannes, France and North America, particularly Miami, San Francisco and New Orleans. In the latter the spicy food gave me a red rash over most parts of my body, and I was placed under observation when passing through New York.

We had obtained the sports catalogue from the American company ESPN, for the territory of Portugal and did surprisingly well. Portugal had joined the European Union and was recovering from years of the Salazar government. There were new TV companies starting up, and the state broadcaster RTP was coming out of its shell.

For my meetings in Portugal I usually took the early flight from Nice to Lisbon and met my TV host at the Lisbon Yacht Club. We then had several days of meetings with him and his staff before I departed for Nice with my order. On one occasion, the owner of Daro, the company I represented, accompanied me to Portugal. Unfortunately, our Air France flight was grounded in Madrid and we could not continue. Pierre, my boss, stood up in the plane and shouted that Air France was a fucking disgrace. A stewardess asked him to leave the plane. He refused. Ground staff appeared, and he still refused. The captain was called from the cockpit and opened the door into the passenger area. As he entered, the door slammed shut, knocking his hat off, and he fell to the ground. All the passengers exploded with laughter, and Pierre refused to move. Eventually the police took us all off the aircraft. So much for help from the boss. Many years later, I was to spend time in Portugal trying to buy a football club and start a pay TV station. At that time, 1998, Portugal was the last country in Europe without pay TV.

In complete contrast to Africa and Portugal was Scandinavia, comprised of Denmark, Sweden, Norway, Finland and Iceland. The Scandinavians were interested in all types of programmes, but buyers needed time to get to know me before becoming loyal, particularly Iceland. The Icelandic buyers wanted me to arrive on Thursday morning and stay until Sunday morning. Weekend drinking was part of their culture, and in the early 1990s, beer was not available in Iceland, and so it was a prized gift. But what a country to visit, with its daily four climates, open air swimming, mud pools, bananas growing in super-heated greenhouses, and amazing fish, as well as whale, to eat. My Icelandic clients played their part and always bought products from me.

The Finns were my next best clients and seemed to have inherited their business genes from their Russian heritage. Finland was part of Russia until December 1917. Even when new companies sprang up, they worked together fairly to decide which company was going to take a certain package of product. One day, I was driving the Finnish buyers around Cannes in the company Mercedes while they decided who was going to buy a package of movies. Eventually, they told me to stop and a spokesman told me who was the winner! Great way to do business! After business in Helsinki, we all took the booze cruise to Tallinn in Estonia. All drink was duty free, and the cruise lasted about eighteen hours. Some very sore heads after this!

Sales in Sweden and Denmark were hard to achieve as too many committees met before decisions were made. In contrast, the Norwegians liked my children's shows and bought large quantities. However, I was shocked one day to receive a call from the Norwegian buyer saying she thought the bear in episode eight of one of my shows was gay, and not suitable for young children. I assured her that there were no gay bears.

Life in Monaco, and of course nearby France, continued with trips to Paris to see clients who always wanted to ogle the nude dancers at the Crazy Horse nightclub. France was coming to the end of its golden economic years, but Monaco, with its booming tax-free status, was still doing well. Every year Monaco hosted the Winter Circus or Cirque d'Hiver, and on one occasion I produced the event for television. We sold the event worldwide to great acclaim.

My circle of friends in Monaco and the surrounding areas slowly increased, and we were invited to attend a weekly session in Vence of The Course in Miracles, a New Age, more human approach to life that dealt with the healing of body, mind and spirit.

A fascinating group got together once a week at the home of an American/Indian couple. Clearly, many of the participants needed healing in one way or the other. The Course in Miracles was open to all comers, and one evening a new participant, called Richard Starkey, arrived. Of course, Ringo Starr was recognised by some Miracle members, and he enjoyed the evening and gave several ladies a lift back to Monaco, where he lived.

Sadly, my wife Pat returned to live in Botswana, and against my wishes took the children with her. I was left alone for some time before Maud decided to give up her job and join me in Monaco. Immigration formalities gave us severe problems for about eighteen months and Maud was constantly threatened with deportation. Eventually, we decided to get married and give Maud status as the wife of a UK citizen. France and Monaco wanted too many papers and certificates, so we went to my hometown of Bristol in the UK and got married in August 1992. Within days, Maud needed to return to South Africa, so my father joked that we had our honeymoon in a layby on the M4 motorway bound for London Heathrow.

Fun and games continued in Monaco and France. The owner of the company slipped on dog shit on a Monaco street as he prepared to take our ancient Mercedes to Cannes for the TV festival. He then suffered the ignominy of breaking down in the middle of Cannes, surrounded by festival participants who knew him well from his trick of filling each person's glass with one bottle of white wine and expecting them to drink it!

I had a verbal agreement with the owner of the company, giving me a ten percent share of the business if I significantly increased his turnover. I fulfilled this goal, so towards the end of 1993, I asked Pierre, the owner, to formalise the agreement. He was not happy and dragged his heels. Despite the intervention of a lawyer, nothing happened. Suddenly, totally unexpectedly, Mnet, my previous South African company, contacted me. They had bought a company based in Amsterdam called Filmnet. Would I like to rejoin them as head of sport for the whole group, including South Africa, and senior vice president for new projects? I discussed this with Maud and her only objection was leaving sunny South of France for grey Holland. It was April 1994, just as South Africa was going through its monumental change and installing Nelson Mandela as president.

For about two months, we lived in the Crowne Plaza Hotel, near Schiphol Airport, Amsterdam. Maud, being a black South African journalist, was anxious to get back to her country to vote for the first time and witness the handover to Nelson Mandela.

I was left alone at the hotel for some weeks. Soon I needed to start commuting to Greece as my first project was starting a Greek pay television network. At that point, Greece was one of the few countries without one. I began commuting between the grey spring of Holland to the beautiful sunny spring of Athens, a back and forth that was to continue until the end of 1994.

The first task was to find premises as we initially worked from our hotel in downtown Athens. Eventually, we found a good site with offices and potential studio space above a garage in north Athens. Then the fun began. Business in Greece is tricky, with the Greeks believing contracts are just the starting point of a business relationship — not the conclusion! Local TV channels fought back, programme suppliers said they would only work through Greek agents who suddenly appeared on the scene, our channel licence was offered to us by fraudulent agents, our first transmitter on the hill outside Athens got destroyed and Maud, my wife, was pursued in the street by Greek men making lurid suggestions.

The key to the success of the channel was a pay TV deal for Greek soccer. Initially, the Greek soccer club owners played hardball and refused to meet. My secretary said we should get an article into the local Athens paper saying we were fed up and would return to Amsterdam and abandon the project. Suddenly, a messenger appeared, saying the league wanted to meet me. Our discussions began.

Many of the top teams in Greece at the time were owned by businessmen who allegedly used their involvement as a front for illegal businesses. These men were difficult to deal with, and during our final decisive meeting, shouted at and insulted me. I told our Greek translator to say in Greek I thought they were a bunch of fucking idiots. The chairman of our Greek company, the former minister of agriculture, was horrified. He was even more distraught when I woke him up at five a.m. to say we had agreed to a deal for five million US dollars and he had to sign a preliminary agreement for both Greece and Cyprus since we also had Cypriot partners.

The next day we met the league again to iron out the fixture list and confirm the competing teams. As predicted, some of the teams already wanted to have their own discussions but this was smoothed out, and we looked forward to the first game which was to be broadcast from a beautiful town in northern Greece called Thessalonica.

Before that, the channel had to officially come to the air. The day the launch happened the studios were surrounded by armed soldiers. Apparently, we had not obtained the correct licence! See what I mean about Greece and contracts?

After lengthy negotiations, we transacted the proper licence, and we had a wonderful opening party in a Greek restaurant with Carla Bruni, now Mrs Sarkozy, and the Gypsy Kings as the stars. Straight from the party, I flew to Thessalonica for the first soccer game, having sent my broadcast truck by road to the venue. For some reason I felt there would be satellite problems that day as this was Greece after all. For insurance, I had engaged an independent warzone satellite operator with a backpack to join me at the venue. As I guessed, the Greek post office had refused our satellite booking, to sabotage our event. But because of my anticipation, there were no problems with pictures and sound! One more obstacle occurred — we had no generator for the truck! How could they forget, and the stadium had no close power source. Someone suggested a lawn mower could help, but eventually a generator was miraculously found in town. The game started, and our studio in Athens was amazed to see the unexpected signal. We had managed the first game but problems continued for some time including the firing of rockets and flares at our cameramen by rival TV stations.

By the end of 1994, we had recruited a hundred local staff of great quality and affluence. Some even bought their own parking spaces in nearby garages. Greece was launched and ran very successfully for the next fifteen years. At the same time, Eastern Europe was waking up from its communist slumber, and besides Greece, I was also flying from Athens to Warsaw to oversee the beginning of our channel in Poland. These were long days flying from Athens to Warsaw and back, trying to secure the Polish soccer league. Warsaw was still a grim city, and only the best hotels had international telephone systems. We stayed at the Hotel Bristol, only to find our rivals Canal Plus in the same building. We quickly left as we were afraid they had bribed the operators to listen to our phone conversations!

Meanwhile, back in Holland, we moved from our rented house in Haarlem and its flooded cellar to a home in the wooded village of Heemstede with a magnificent, elevated street full of small, but high-quality shops. The house was just behind a bulb farm, blooming with its magnificent flowers in the spring. My main job was to put together sports content deals for the growing number of channels we owned in Scandinavia, Benelux, Italy, Greece, Poland, and South Africa. We were also assembling deals with the Kirsch organisation in Germany and ITV in the UK. In fact, we came close to buying the UK Premier League with ITV in an attempt to block the Murdoch organisation invading Europe and possibly Africa. We also fought off an attempt to start a new sports channel in Holland by purchasing programme rights together with the state broadcaster NOS.

In June 1995, South Africa reached the final of the Rugby World Cup for the first time. I was in Johannesburg for the game as head of sport for the whole company. Russell MacMillan, then sport chief for the South African part of the business, had negotiated deals for South African Rugby. Unknown to him, the rugby authorities of South Africa, Australia and New Zealand were planning to turn rugby into a fully professional game, with clubs and countries from the southern hemisphere competing against each other on an annual basis. The shift would be the beginning of Super Rugby as we know it today. If the move went forward, all our southern hemisphere rugby contracts would be null and void, and we would be under attack from Murdoch if he wished to enter the African market.

At the end of the World Cup tournament, I persuaded the Mnet/Multichoice management in Johannesburg to try and stop the formation of Super Rugby. We knew that the South African players were very unhappy with the lack of consultation with the contracts they were being offered. Indeed Francois Pienaar, the Springbok captain, lost his job as he stood up for the players and relocated to London. A chance meeting in Johannesburg with James Erskine, the IMG Australian representative visiting South Africa for the World Cup, persuaded me to talk to Michael Lynagh, the Australian rugby captain, to see if we could persuade the Aussie team not to join the Super Rugby circus. Obviously with only the Kiwis and the Boks there could be no southern hemisphere Super Rugby. By then, Michael Lynagh had returned to Australia. I flew back to Amsterdam and then onto Sydney, Australia to meet the Australian rugby captain and his agent, James Erskine.

At the time, the Murdoch organisation was reputed to be offering six hundred million US dollars for a ten-year deal to get Super Rugby going. The rugby unions in the three nations were receiving no more than three million each per season, so it was obvious that the administrators craved a deal. Rugby in Australia hardly made the top ten of most watched sports, and was regarded as weak financially.

I met Michael Lynagh at a restaurant in the Sydney suburb of Paddington on two occasions to thrash out a deal he could put to his players. Basically, we categorised the players into groupings of A, B and C in terms of value, and would offer them a certain sum of money not to play for three years. This reward for not playing amounted to approximately twelve million US dollars, or four million per annum.

We were aware that there was another strategy put forward by Ross Turnbull, a former player, and probably funded by the Packer organisation, although James Packer denied this. I pressed on and tried to get the American sports network ESPN involved, so eventually they could control Super Rugby rights in other parts of the world. Regretfully, they were unwilling to commit. I phoned the company management in South Africa and explained that for twelve million US dollars, we could remove the Australian team from Super Rugby, still control our own South African rugby rights, and negotiate separately with the Kiwis. Maybe CEO Koos Bekker was having other conversations with other parties, along with Russell MacMillan, head of sport in South Africa, and they decided not to back my plan. I shall never know why.

The result was in 1996, the first Super 12 season, which was won by Auckland Blues. The Super 12 was a nineteen-year deal between the three nations, Sanzar, and News Corp, the ultimate owner of the competition. The contract gave all broadcast rights to Super 12, Tri Nations, games, all land tours, and test matches in Australia, South Africa and New Zealand, as well as provincial matches. The deal was north of five hundred and fifty million US dollars! The South African share was estimated to be two hundred million. From 2010, the agreement extended to five years with the Sanzar Unions paying four hundred and thirty-seven million.

Life continued in Holland as we had moved into a pleasant home in Heemstede, a cycle ride from the sea and pleasant drive across the canals to work. We also enjoyed three wonderful summers with the sun shining until almost eleven p.m. Holland is a well-organised country with many attractions and things to do. It was the only country I lived in where your will was published nationally within two hours, and the town hall knew instantly your new address when you moved.

We were buying sports rights at a fast rate, and setting up channels throughout Europe. Our financial backers were getting anxious, and discussions had been ongoing with DIRECTV in America for a buyout. Then the incredible happened: on the day DIRECTV were due to sign, Canal Plus from France entered the arena and concluded a buyout of the company's TV activities worldwide, apart from Greece and South Africa. My hopes of working for DIRECTV in the USA fell apart, and eventually Canal Plus forced me to leave my position. Within weeks in June 1997, my father passed away in Bristol, and I spent the next six months sorting out his affairs and preparing to leave Holland in February 1998.

It had been an incredible journey so far. Able to watch overspill British TV in Holland, I had become aware of happenings in the UK after my absence of nearly twenty years: the end of the Major years in government and the rise of Tony Blair in politics; the tragic death of Princess Diana on Aug 31, 1997; the end of Irish problems with the signing of the Belfast agreement in April 1998; the curious incident of the film donation to the Labour Party by Bernie Ecclestone of Formula 1. I was dealing with Mr E. at the time, and he told me how the Japanese rights holders of Formula 1 had asked for a reduction in their fees upon the death of favourite driver Ayrton Senna. Bernie said he told them he would try and bring him back!

In 1998, Amazon launched in the UK, and we saw the rise of the iconic David Beckham, the Millennium Dome and the London Eye, and also in 1998, reminding me of Bristol, we saw the last bombsite cleared for development.

In Holland, 'Big Brother' came on the air and the format swept the world, as did the internet and mobile phones. I had got my first mobile in 1995. After Diana's death, the BBC set up a full online news service, and it became the UK's most visited site.

We moved to France and the UK for a period while I prepared, at age fifty-three, for life as an independent consultant. Unknown to me, the future held a directorship at Leeds United Football club, consultancy in Japan, a boxing promoters' licence, and sponsorship of the African Cup of Nations and much more!

We finally left Holland in February 1998 after four wonderful years. We sold our house and some furniture was sent to our French address; the rest was put into storage in Amsterdam. We did not know where we would finish our journey. I had a short-term consultancy contract with Canal Plus in France, but knew that Jerome Valcke, deputy head of sport in Paris, was determined to get rid of me. I earned too much and knew too much. After six months the contract was not renewed, and Canal Plus took over the sports department in Holland. Jerome Valcke eventually became general secretary for FIFA and has since been banned from the business for ten years. Maud and I decided to rent an apartment in Notting Hill. There were many sports companies in London, and friends.

One of my friends, Mike Murphy, whose company sold the 1991 World Cup Rugby rights, suggested I join the East India Club in London's St. James Square. The club could be my London pied-à-terre. Or somewhere to put your feet up, said Murphy. The East India Club happened to be the headquarters of the International Rugby Board, now World Rugby, so Murphy had no problem with approval for my membership.

I easily bought tickets for games at Twickenham, and spent many a merry Saturday in a car park enjoying beer and pork pies before the game started. Mike Murphy was a pioneer in TV, sports broadcasting and a former editor of the BBC's Grandstand sports show — a very kind man with a great address book, who sadly passed away in 2003 from cancer at the age of fifty-one. Mike was a London Irishman, and I am sure would have appreciated the irony of dying in Dublin amongst friends and family.

At the age of fifty-three, I was out in the market looking for work and receiving interview opportunities with the Premier League, English Rugby Union, Nigerian Television etc., all at the same time. Greg Dyke, later to become the boss of the BBC, but at that time CEO of Pearson, also put me in touch with several companies. Greg was a director of Manchester United at that time, and I had just joined the board of Leeds United. But more of that later.

I was in Bristol, staying with an uncle, when out of the blue, I got a phone call from DIRECTV in America. I knew them from my Monaco days when I sold them programmes for their new pay TV channels in America. Stephanie Campbell, now DIRECTV Director of Programmes, had suggested my name to the executives of the company as a person who could advise on the purchase of sports programmes in Japan and assist in cancelling a contract with Formula 1 and Mr Ecclestone.

DIRECTV was already in Japan, and one of their local shareholders had gone ahead without board permission to negotiate a deal with Formula 1, for two hundred and fifty US dollars. The American shareholders were furious. I set off for Japan and worked in that fascinating country for more than two years. At the time, DIRECTV was owned by Hughes Aircraft Corporation and there were frequent visits from executives in Los Angeles who would visit Tokyo for two or three days, make major decisions and leave the local US and Japanese staff to carry them out. There were some stunning American staff who spoke and wrote Japanese and some great engineers but curiously the Americans seemed afraid of the Japanese co-owners and failed to make major marketing and content decisions.

The young son of one of the Japanese shareholders of DIRECTV had, without board permission, contacted Bernie Ecclestone and verbally agreed a huge deal to take Formula 1 motor car racing away from the then incumbent Fuji TV. The Hughes executives wanted the deal to be stopped, but were afraid Ecclestone would sue them for damages. I took the young Japanese gentleman to London to explain the situation to Mr E. The young man spoke no English, so with an interpreter we entered Mr Ecclestone's office, just off Hyde Park. Bernie looked at him and told him to get out. Not even good morning. The Japanese fellow understood the tone and of course the translation!

We left the office bewildered and returned to our hotel. Later in the afternoon, Mr Ecclestone's office phoned to say he would meet the Japanese entourage at his club that evening, in Mayfair. During the dinner, Mr Ecclestone agreed to let the proposed deal fall away. No doubt he had used the bid to get a higher bid from Fuji TV. DIRECTV was delighted, and my consultancy continued for another eighteen months or so. Deals were struck to reduce the price of baseball productions, a local world title boxing match was screened, and negotiations began for the World Cup soccer tournament to be staged in Japan and Korea in 2002.

I enjoyed Japanese food and often went to Japanese-only restaurants, ordering from the pictures on the menu since no one spoke English. Japanese restaurant owners found us interesting and amusing and would applaud when I ate something a bit strange. Unfortunately, I did not like the kimchi food in South Korea, and like my crew who covered the World Cup in 2002, avoided it and ended up in TGIF (Thank God It's Friday) most days.

The World Cup deal for the tournament in 2002 in Japan and Korea, and 2006 in Germany, became available to us for about six hundred million US dollars. All rights, exclusive to us in Japan, with the possibility to sell on to NHK, the Japanese state broadcaster. This deal would have really put us on the map in Japan. The local executives were overjoyed, but the Americans were frightened of offending the Japanese in their own country. This situation, and the potential change of ownership of DIRECTV in USA, meant that the deal eventually remained unsigned. Such a pity as I am sure DIRECTV would have captured the market instead of eventually joining up with Sky Perfect TV.

Japan had good relations with Brazil and Italy. Both soccer leagues were important in Japan, as was Italian food, which shares characteristics with Japanese food. In Brazil, there were more than one million citizens of Japanese descent who had free right of access to Japan. Yet Korean families, who date from the Japanese occupation of Korea, are still discriminated against, and children of mixed couples where particularly the mother is Japanese, can't get Japanese nationality. The latter abuse upset many of the Americans from DIRECTV.

My work continued in Japan until late 2001, but in 1997 I had been approached to become a non-executive director of Leeds United soccer team. My friend Chris Akers, formerly of Credit Suisse, then my consultant in Holland, had assembled a group of banks to finance the deal for thirty million pounds. I was to become the director in charge of remuneration and television deals. Unusual twins! Leeds had just won the last Division One title before the Premier League began. Free of duties in Holland, I was able to devote time to this famous club.

Chris had dismissed Howard Wilkinson as manager and had brought in George Graham to replace him. George was returning after a sabbatical for taking money from transfer deals at Arsenal. He was told to find players, and the director would do the financial deals in future. The club at the time was in chaos, needing new players and new administrative management. But it had great potential and great history. Manchester United recommended a CEO who started well but eventually proved to be not good enough. He upset Leeds Town Council and eventually was dismissed by Chris Akers, the chairman, in a flood of tears and a promise he could keep his Range Rover.

We intended to expand the stadium and add a railway station at the ground. The stadium was bought back from the city council, which pleased the rate payers, and the ground staff, who could now return the grass to its former glory. George Graham turned Lucas Radebe from South Africa into a top player with personal coaching and bought in strong players Jimmy Floyd Hasselbaink and Alf-Inge Haaland. The latter would tackle anything, including the corner post, and eventually had his career ended by Roy Keane who avenged a previous tackle and broke Alf's leg. George Graham, who always dressed immaculately, sat with directors during the first forty-five minutes and shouted into the phone linked to the dugout. The second half, dressed in his suit, he was on the touchline talking to the players. If the team played well he would always talk to the directors, if not he disappeared with the players.

On the pitch, Leeds started to do well and were often close to the top of the table during our ownership.

Unfortunately, all was not well amongst the directors, and a local director called Peter Ridsdale caused trouble at the board meetings and ousted Chairman Chris Akers. Within months, the other directors left, and I was contracted in early 1999 by Leicester City to advise their board on a solution to their internal problems, and try and prevent their highly successful manager, Martin O'Neill, from leaving the club.

Martin had been told Leeds had a huge pot of transfer money available to spend if he went to the northern powerhouse. The claim was not true, of course, and I told Martin this fact. He did not leave for Leeds, but instead finished his contract and left for Celtic in 2000, to be replaced by Peter Taylor. My contract was terminated at Leicester, and a new board was appointed with a new stadium in the pipeline. Soccer clubs are difficult to manage; the pressure from fans, shareholders, players, and agents is intense. Everybody has a viewpoint. At one of the Leeds United AGMs, we made the mistake of having George Graham on the platform with the directors. Suddenly a shareholder stood up and said our left back was hopeless, and his mother could play better. George tried to answer but was shouted down. In future George was never at the AGM, but always far away with the players.

I had been juggling my consultancies with DIRECTV and Leeds and Leicester, but at the same time had been trying to make proper contact with Independent TV or ITV in the UK. The network was moving ahead with a challenge to Sky TV and aiming to set up a pay TV bouquet of channels. This operation was ultimately to go bankrupt in March 2002.

Unknown to most people, the South African/Dutch based company I had just left had been collaborating with ITV and the Kirch organisation in Germany for the purpose of buying sports rights on a worldwide basis. Indeed Kirch, through the efforts of the remarkable Dr Dieter Hahn, managed to purchase World Cup soccer rights on a worldwide basis. The Kirch Group also owned substantial TV rights to Formula 1 motor racing. The person I had been dealing with at ITV was Malcolm Wall, a former Harlequins rugby player, and now CEO of United Broadcasting, which owned the last TV channels of the ITV group not belonging to Granada. United channels were concentrated in Wales and the south of the UK.

Unknown to many people, Mnet, now Multichoice in South Africa, and its European affiliates had also worked in the late 1990s with ITV Sports Group headed by Malcolm Wall, to bid for the UK Premier League rights for the UK, Europe and sub-Saharan Africa. ITV wanted the Premier League rights to block Sky TV in the UK. We wanted to ensure our number one sports rights in our European territories, and to show Murdoch he could not get into Africa. He had already taken control of Super Rugby and leased it back to us. Anyway, the deal failed because ITV wanted a five-year deal with the Premier League, and the club owners would not agree. Makes you wonder what would have happened to Sky if the deal had gone through!

I tracked down Malcolm Wall and found him in Bristol. United Business Media had bought the regional TV channel called HTV in June 1997, and Malcolm had been spending half of his week commuting from London to ensure a smooth transition. He asked me to become CEO of HTV, but having spent fifteen years attending TV meetings, I turned down the opportunity as I wished to have a freer professional role in television.

Malcolm understood and immediately offered me a role as a consultant to the United group. I advised him on all new programming matters, including digital channels and sports acquisitions. United needed some local sport to fulfil their licence requirements and I managed to persuade Malcolm and Jim Raven, his head of news and sport, now a successful crime writer, to programme World Championship boxing around their regions.

I was able to bring Rodney Berman and Golden Gloves from South Africa which had a stable of top-class boxers and several local UK trainers to provide opposition. But first I needed a boxing promoters' licence, and so I faced the interview at the Boxing Board of Control in London. I had no criminal record and answered all their questions about the boxers I would bring to the UK. I received my licence, and from 1999 until late 2001 we produced about twenty tournaments featuring World Championship boxing throughout southern England and Wales. We produced two UK world champions in Glenn Catley and Robert Norton, and even promoted a few events for Sky TV. At an event in Glasgow, the promoter introduced me to his friend, who he described as Scotland's biggest drug dealer. Needless to say, I moved on quickly as I did when one of the UK's top promoters threatened my South African group when he realised his fighter was losing. Those years were very busy for me: Japan, Leeds and ITV consultations.

Outside the UK, Golden Gloves continued to promote other boxing tournaments, and I was fortunate enough to be in South Africa in April 2001 for the World Heavyweight title fight between Lennox Lewis, the champion, and Hasim Rahman. Unprepared, Lennox Lewis lost a KO to Rahman. I also saw an awesome Lewis knock out Tyson in Memphis, USA in 2004 for the undisputed heavyweight title of the world.

Many years later, in Miami, I talked to Lennox about the Rahman knockout, and he admitted he had been taking part in a movie and was not well prepared. But as for the Tyson fight, he was in great shape and very focused.

In mid-2003, I received a phone call from an old friend, Robin Courage, who was promoting the All Africa Games in Abuja, Nigeria in October of that year. He asked me to sell the TV rights on a worldwide basis. After much effort, I managed sales throughout Africa and Europe, and prepared to go to Abuja to meet my clients, many of whom were going to pay me cash. Luckily, we had codes attached to our signals leaving the stadium as some customers tried to steal the signal. We soon blocked them off.

The stadium was new, but the new fleet of BMW cars had virtually disappeared; the food at the new South African owned hotel was inedible; the Wi-Fi was not working, and there was no warning that malaria was in the area. Several athletes, who had not been advised to take precautions, died from malaria.

What we did have was lots of TV equipment, including outside broadcast trucks! Both Sony and Thomson had supplied equipment at the request of highly placed persons, but no one had paid. The result was that both crews refused to work or co-operate with each other. We risked having no pictures and so nothing to sell to clients who had paid, and who had big audiences waiting in their countries. It was also clear that events were rocking Nigeria, as well as the stadium. Someone had to organise the daily programme of televised events and bring in the signals for retransmission. That someone had to be me. So, for the duration of the games, I became the technical director in a hot room for most of the day and eating only boiled rice. Great experience in a town where even the traffic lights on the way to the airport did not work! That was the last time I worked in Nigeria.

Late in 2003, my wife and I decided to travel to India with an old friend called Ron Moodley. He was of Indian-South African descent, and we had worked together in the early days at Mnet in South Africa. Ron had subsequently brought the Indian channel transmitted by Mnet. We had meetings arranged with Indian TV companies and programme makers such as the Sagar family. The Sagars had studios in an area of Mumbai, surrounded by shacks and poverty, producing wonderful programmes such as the epic TV series, Ramayan. This series of seventy-eight episodes was first shown in India in 1987 and 1988 and was a great hit. Subsequently it played throughout the world. The Sagars subsequently built their own Sagar World theme park not far from Mumbai. India, with its colours, smells, poverty, humility, wealth, cricket, noise and cows. Bollywood is indeed a place to visit and produce television.

The world was slipping towards an unseen financial crisis, but new projects were still arriving at my computer. A UK based investor called Julian McIntyre, assisted by Tim Ellis, my former boss at Mnet in South Africa, floated and financed a new channel for sub-Saharan Africa called Gateway Broadcast Services or GTV. He raised approximately two hundred million US dollars in late 2006, but was unable to raise further capital in February 2009, and the service stopped abruptly.

During its short lifetime, GTV created jobs and competition in twenty-two African markets. I was tasked to get the UK Premier League rights for sub-Saharan English-speaking Africa and take them away from Multichoice/DSTV, the incumbent at that time. I succeeded in signing a deal for twenty-eight million US dollars for three seasons. This move was the programming masterstroke for GTV, ensuring the service got a large and growing customer base from the beginning. We also spent large sums of money on the local African soccer leagues, which was a first. Until then local soccer had been ignored in most South African countries.

The service grew very quickly, although customer service was poor and could not cope with demand from twenty-two countries. By early 2009, GTV had more than a hundred and twenty thousand subscribers, but needed more capital to make bids for other programming such as the European Champions League. Investors refused to invest more capital, and to the anger of many subscribers, GTV closed without prior notice in February 2009, leaving many debts. At least I had shown that big rivals could be defeated for content in Africa.

One of the soccer programmes featured on GTV was the Africa Cup of Nations, in essence the African World Cup, but played every two years. I was approached by MTN, one of Africa's largest mobile phone providers, to negotiate for them the lead sponsorship of the event. They wanted it to be known as the MTN Africa Cup of Nations for 2006 and 2008. MTN was trying to expand into Egypt in 2006 and already had a strong foothold in Ghana where the 2008 event was to be held.

In 2006, Cairo and all the main towns where games were to be staged were decked out in yellow, the MTN brand colour. It was a spectacular show everywhere, including along the Nile. Arriving at Cairo Airport is always confusing as there are so many booths issuing visas! Outside, usually friendly taxi drivers often asked me my religion. At that time, it seemed fine to be a Christian, and if my visit coincided with Ramadan there was always much feasting as the sun went down.

Cairo is a spectacular place to visit with its pyramids, river, bustling crowds, restaurants, perfume and papyrus shops, museums, antique shops in people's homes, and dark alleys. Some games were played in Alexandria, a port on the Mediterranean. The town is still beautiful. Once a mixture of people from all over the Middle East and Mediterranean lived in it. The result was a proliferation of excellent restaurants, and gold and textile markets featuring Egyptian cotton. One of the soccer games at the stadium featured the Nigerian team, sponsored by a Nigerian telecoms company. I was with the MTN team and the AFRICAN CUP OF NATIONS executives who noticed a group of several hundred people in the crowd all clothed in green and often featured on camera. A call to the production truck put a stop to this affront, and the green supporters were removed by the stewards.

MTN had also signed for the Africa Cup of Nations sponsorship rights in Ghana for 2008. Telecoms company MTN had a huge presence in Ghana, so their branding was everywhere. Maud and I flew to Accra, as guests of the event organisers. We were met at the airport by a police escort with flashing blue lights and driven to our hotel by the beach. We had tickets for most of the games, and also managed a trip inland where we sampled bush meat, sold to us on the side of the road, and cooked in a nearby restaurant. To my surprise, no stomach problems. We found an upmarket German restaurant in Accra where the owner had his own boat to fish for the catch of the day. The highlight of the trip was the Africa Cup of Nations final at the national stadium. The game was won by Egypt, and I was accosted by a pickpocket as I left the grounds. I realised my wallet had been taken from my pocket and grabbed the thief, who by then had passed my wallet to someone else in the crowd. I pushed the thief against a wall and threatened him. Suddenly I was surrounded by other fans leaving the stadium and the police. After much shouting and pushing, my wallet was returned to me by an apparent onlooker in the crowd. The thief by then had disappeared.

Production opportunities for the soccer World Cup in Germany in 2006 and soccer European Nations Cup in Austria in 2008 led to long stays in both countries.

Memorably, I was threatened by Croatian supporters in Vienna who objected to me working for Middle Eastern TV channels. This was only ten years or so after the end of the Balkan revolution and memories were still raw.

As a freelance consultant, I was always looking to diversify. A friend introduced me to a former major from the British army. He was called Bryson Gifford. This gentleman wanted to set up a security company to look after high-net-worth individuals throughout the world. So together we set up Stonehouse Security. South Africa had been awarded the FIFA Soccer World Cup for 2010, and we knew many wealthy and famous persons wished to visit and be well protected. As Stonehouse CEO, Bryson Gifford found offices and partners in South Africa, and we recruited locally based experienced operatives from many parts of the continent. In fact, Africa is and was awash with former soldiers who had access to guns and knew how to look after important people such as presidents and former politicians.

Our operatives picked up clients at airports, transported them to various locations for games and ensured they departed safely. Many rich Americans wanted discreet guarding, whilst billionaire Russians brought their own men, who needed our armed services while in South Africa. Top footballers, working as commentators for television, usually wanted transport to games, restaurants and night clubs. We had no real incidents in South Africa, apart from the theft of one of our vehicles by a staff member. Our success in Africa led to a contract with a Russian company to protect the Russian Pavilions in Hyde Park, London, during the 2012 Olympic Games. Our team comprised many retired UK marines and former SAS members who did a great job, despite our Russian client's constant interference and penny pinching. However, we also helped a French company with protection work, and despite a visit to Paris by some of our ex-SAS staff, they refused to pay us in full. Needless to say their inability to pay ensured they did not work again!

My wife's cousin had become the chairman of Armscor South Africa, the body controlling the purchasing of arms for South Africa and the sale of South African arms to the rest of the world. A friend in Turkey controlled a television content business and also specialised in supplying arms to the Turkish military. The cousin asked for an introduction to my friend as at that time relations between Turkey and South Africa were not good. I put the meeting together in Istanbul in early 2008. Discussions were good but deals were not concluded at that time. However, my Turkish friend entertained me well and took me to an exclusive night club on the Bosphorus. Just about every top person, apart from the president, was in the club that evening. A splendid buffet was provided, and then my friend suggested we call his driver to visit his house in Asia on the other side of the river for another party. As we got into the car, my acquaintance gave me a gun and told me to fire if anybody tried to stop us. I asked him why, and he told me as an arms dealer his life was always in danger. Luckily, we reached his house without incident and I handed the gun to the guard at the gate. The rest of the evening was splendid, and I returned safely to France next day.

Life continued with the advent of digital rights for sport and the arrival of new channels in Africa presenting a challenge. The influence of the Chinese on the African TV landscape was also very noticeable. My wife and children were now living in South Africa full time, and so I commuted between Europe and Africa and occasionally visited other countries such as the USA, Canada and Singapore.

I have now been living in Africa for more than forty years. During that time I have kept in touch with a group of friends who went to primary school and grammar school with me. Incredibly, we have remained close for nearly sixty-five years. Slowly, we have begun to have more funerals than weddings. So, to Jim, Roger, Andrew known as Tub, Garth, Brian, Steve, Peter known as Phred, and their ladies past and present, a big thank you for your love and kindness. The same to my wonderful wife and children.

I hope I live long enough to see democracy survive in Africa and buy at an auction a 1901 edition of the Tailor of Gloucester where it all started.

P.S. Just discovered as my book goes to press I have another branch of the family, the Saunders. My cousin left me an inheritance, and this opened the lid on the branch of my mother's, mother's family centred on Uncle Harold. This branch of the family is just as outrageous as the other. Uncle Harold, despite his age, sailed a boat to Dunkirk in May 1940 to rescue British soldiers trapped on the beach. One of his nieces abandoned her two children on Victoria Station in London and was last heard of in Peru.

To cap it all I was diagnosed with cancer, recovered and needed a hernia operation. The surgeon warned me I could lose a testicle, but no need to worry as even at seventy I would be able to father children.